W9-CSS-583

SECRETS
OF OFFSHORE
TAX HAVENS

ROBERT CHAPPELL

SECRETS OF OFFSHORE TAX HAVENS

Copyright © 1985

First Printing November 1985
Second Printing April 1986

ABM PUBLISHING CO.

ISBN 0-9614774-0-7

Cataloging in Publication Data

Chappell, Robert 1934 -
   Secrets of offshore tax havens.
   1. Investments, Foreign. 2. Tax shelters. 3. Taxation of
foreign investments. I. Title.
                 332.673

Cover by Jay Wegter

Printed in the United States of America

In Athens, it was customary to rob rich citizens of a part of their wealth, though one used an honourable excuse.

George Wilhelm Hegel
German Philosopher, 1770-1831

Acknowledgments

Special thanks to the following for their support and encouragement...

Lindsey, Keith, Carson, Mickey, Nelly,

Dicey, Earl, John, Faye, Rose, Tom, Joe,

Robert and Doris, Marc, Barry, and Anne

Table of Contents

About The Author

Robert Chappell is one of the world's foremost authorities on offshore tax haven jurisdictions and a well-known expert for many years in the field of professional estate planning for individual United States taxpayers.

He is the founder and president of Nassau Life Insurance Company, Ltd., which has executive quarters in Nassau, the capital of the Bahamas and an international financial center. Home offices are located in the Turks and Caicos Islands, a British crown colony close to Nassau and Miami. He was previously the founder and president of a brokerage firm, an investment company and a life insurance company in the United States.

The author has lived in Europe and traveled extensively to research the history and the current laws of tax havens throughout Europe as well as other important tax haven jurisdictions located around the world. He has also lived in the Turks and Caicos Islands and is one of the leading authorities on the laws and practices of tax haven jurisdictions found in the Atlantic-Caribbean region.

In recent years the author has written extensively and been a featured speaker throughout the United States on the advantages in tax savings to be realized through legal use of offshore tax havens by individual U.S. taxpayers. He is also the director of an ongoing series of specialized tax saving and estate planning seminars conducted at the internationally famous Rock Sound Club in the Bahamas and attended by private business owners and individual taxpayers from throughout the world.

The author's work with noted attorneys who are experts in U.S. tax laws has resulted in significant legal opinions and U.S. tax court decisions that have set new precedents in protecting the rights of American taxpayers who utilize offshore trust arrangements that until now seemed the exclusive domain of the super-rich.

Preface

Perhaps the greatest form of torture—the greatest plague, the greatest burden, the greatest source of high blood pressure, heart attack, depression and mental anguish—ever imposed upon a nation is the so-called voluntary income tax of the United States of America. It is an agonizing burden which is always there. The filing of one tax return is barely completed when one must start thinking about the next return. Hardly a business decision can be made without considering the tax implications above the economic, business and common sense factors.

One never knows whether he has "done it right" to the extent that he will not have his property confiscated or his freedom threatened. The fact of innocence or guilt is of little consequence since the taxpayer can be ruined financially, his family split and lost by merely having to defend himself against charges of not paying enough, of fraud, and in essence of having done it wrong. Attorneys and certified public accountants can use all of a person's liquid assets and force the sale of others to cover the horrendous cost of defense of actions they or their associates approved and sanctioned.

This condition is not something an outside enemy did to the American people. They, in a democratic society, did it to themselves. One can distinguish little difference between a totalitarian system, wherein the torturer appoints himself, and one wherein the "torturees" appoint their own torturer through their democratic processes.

A democratic totalitarian system, such as the present system of the United States, produces the same effect as the communistic totalitarian system. The end result is the same: misery for the citizens, total control, a deprivation of motivation and creativity and a false sense of priorities wherein resources are directed toward bombs, rockets, pesticides and geoengineering which threaten man's very existence on his own planet.

No one could very effectively deny that one devilish young man named Karl Marx, who had just received his doctorate under the teaching of the famous philosopher George Wilhelm Hegel, has brought about his stated desire:

> To change everything existing by turning Hegel
> upside down.

Russia bought Marx's theories of a central money-flow system totally. The USA bought half of it with the intention of going all the way.

Marx convinced the world that only through allowing all of a man's production to flow through a central government, with committees to determine what he was to receive back, could the individual attain dignity and a fair deal from his existence.

Marx used devious and deceitful theories such as "estrangement" to sell his philosophy, i.e., "...the more perfect a worker makes his product the more deformed he sees himself in a capitalistic free enterprise system." And, "When a worker produces a product for a private entrepreneur he is estranged from his product when he has to turn it over to his boss, thereby losing his dignity."

Marx turned all of man's natural evolution which had occurred from his beginning into a *man*-directed or *state*-directed godless society. That is what the income tax system is all about: directing, dominating and controlling not only factors of production, but also every aspect of every person's existence.

Marx and his followers reasoned that man's essence for existence came from existence itself and not from an external plan, superior being, or God. Therefore, mankind should and could control all aspects of his existence through communism or democratic socialism.

It is this control and domination contained in the tax system to which I object. Milton Friedman, the Nobel laureate, has said, "Without a great measure of economic freedom no other freedom can be had." Marx and his followers made their attack in the right place—the economy—to accomplish their ends, i.e., total control.

Once the system was in place, the agency or bureaucracy known as the Internal Revenue Service (IRS) could be used to control not only judges, governors and presidents, but congressmen and senators as well. Little more would be necessary to defeat a legislator or public office seeker than a leak to the press that the candidate is under investigation by the IRS. Legislators and public office holders must also live in fear of the IRS. Their future, to a great extent, is in the hands of the IRS. The burden, the mental agonies or disease, are definitely there, and perhaps for a long time into the future.

The problem is that because of ambiguities in the tax code, the different interpretations of tax practitioners, and the variety of positions the IRS can take on any issue, there is no way, within the system, that one can "do it right" to the extent that he could be certain that he will not be audited, penalized, indicted and imprisoned. This is a fine position for a nation of people to have placed themselves! Therefore, new ways must be sought.

It would make little sense to argue that mankind would be in a better position had Karl Marx not successfully turned Hegel upside down. But one could make a persuasive argument that advancements were occurring rapidly under the private free enterprise system that allowed Thomas Alva Edison, Henry Ford, the Wright brothers, Alexander Graham Bell and other great Americans to exercise their God-given talents.

The great German philosopher Kant, who was Hegel's teacher, is credited with developing the science of transcendence. Hopefully, the concept of the Contractual Company, which I have developed with Kant's transcendence theories in mind, will enable a great number of enslaved people to *transcend* the chains of the governmental restrictions that bring misery to their existence. (The concept of the Contractual Company will be revealed in this book.) Hopefully, people will regain the God-given motivation, creativity and freedom necessary not only to serve society but to find peace of mind and a measure of happiness, fulfillment, security and dignity for themselves.

Hegel's science of phenomenology will be utilized to consider tax havens and tax avoidance from many points of view. Perhaps those people who are able to transcend our present problems can bring just change, turn Marx upside down and set the world upon an upright course again.

Chapter I

The New Economy

Effective tax planning is becoming more critical to survival as we witness the breaking down of all our institutions and the enormous changes in a 50-year-old economy that is rapidly being replaced by a new economy. Those who prepare themselves to cope with this new economy will survive, even prosper. Those who continue to arrange their affairs in the same old ways are the people who will become the innocent victims of the new economy.

What will life be like in the post-industrial western societies? The answer is obviously that no one knows because it is a state of being where no one has been before. However, it is clear that life will be different than we can visualize through the remainder of this century and the first decades of the next. At the same time, if we recognize where we are in this process of change, we can have a realistic chance to prepare for the future.

The present, or old and dying, economy was in essence born in 1934 with a mass of new legislation involving banking, securities, and taxation. That economy has lived its 50-year cycle.

I have long believed in the cycle, or wave, theory of economic history. Only by examining the history of world economics, one in which great waves of prosperity are followed by long periods of decline and even depression, can we see the futility of shortsighted economists and politicians who try to save a dying economy with desperate remedies.

The founder of the long-wave theory was Nikolai Kondratieff, a ranking scholar at Moscow's Agricultural Academy.
He died in the 1930s in one of Stalin's Siberian prison camps,
sent there because he dared to dispute the Marxist doctrine.
In the early 1920s Kondratieff had begun studying 100-year-
plus series of commodity prices for France, Britain and the
rapidly growing United States. He was struck by a pattern
in which price indices rose sharply, then fell sharply, then
rose again and fell again with remarkable regularity.

In 1926, in one of his rare published works, Kondratieff
described what today's economists still study as the long-
wave theory:

> The upswing of the first long wave embraces
> the period from 1789 to 1814, i.e. 25 years; its
> decline begins in 1814 and ends in 1849, a period
> of 35 years. The cycle is, therefore, completed in
> 60 years.
>
> The rise of the second wave begins in 1849 and
> ends in 1873, lasting 24 years. The decline of the
> second wave begins in 1873 and ends in 1896, a
> period of 23 years. The length of the second wave
> is 47 years.
>
> The upward movement of the third wave begins
> in 1896 and ends in 1920, its duration being 24
> years. The decline of the wave, according to all
> data, begins in 1920.[1]

British economic historian E. H. Phelps Brown went even
further back in history than Kondratieff, tracing the patterns
of English prices and wages all the way back to 1254. "What
we found," he said, "is not cycles but patterns. What we
can learn from patterns is that economic history has its
phases. From the end of the Second World War we were

---

[1] *Forbes*, November 9, 1981.

catching up with the technology that came out of that war, and that catching up was a major stimulus to investment. Today that particular characteristic is pretty well worked out. You cannot build a third railroad between two towns and you cannot put a third refrigerator in the average home."[2]

As I stated earlier, the present U.S. economy was actually born out of the new banking, securities and taxation legislation of 1934. That started a new wave of prosperity in America, carried to its highest crest by the post-war economy. But if we follow the long-wave theory, that economy has reached the end of its 50-year cycle. It is, in other words, a dying economy rapidly being replaced by history's next wave. How well we prepare to meet this newest wave will determine whether we ride it out and prosper, or become engulfed by it and drown in economic depressions.

These are some of my views of our future:

Big government, big business and big labor will fail. Not only the cry for freedom, but economic necessity will bring on thousands of small, new enterprises working on an independent contractor basis in all areas of endeavor. These enterprises will be relying on economic laws and God-given principles of survival with less faith in statutory rules and regulations as the rules become more restrictive and destructive to the individual and to society as a whole.

Not one of man's major institutions is serving him well at present. Many of the major manufacturing companies are technically bankrupt, owing more in pension commitments than their total net worth. Insurance companies are so bound up in rules, regulations, and paperwork that their effectiveness is hampered.

Banks and savings and loans are failing at the highest rate since the Great Depression. State and federal banking regulators closed 79 banks in 1984 and more than 40 banks had

---

[2]*Ibid.*

gone under during the first quarter of 1985, when one out of every 16 federally insured banks was on the "problem" list kept by the Federal Deposit Insurance Corporation (FDIC).[3] Runs on savings and loans were forcing state governments to declare bank holidays. Dozens of thrifts failed and others scrambled to stay alive by merging while record numbers were on the brink of insolvency.

Government takes so much money away from the individual that there is not enough discretionary income left to sustain healthy capital markets. There are not enough small investors in the world for the big institutions to rely upon for liquidity. Therefore, all of these large institutions must rely upon current income to meet commitments.

Ownership of stock brokerage firms is changing faster than Hollywood marriages. Mergers of old, reliable firms are occurring continuously. Giant E. F. Hutton, so respected that everyone was supposed to stop and listen when E. F. Hutton talked, is caught in a massive check-kiting scheme. A *New York Times* story is headlined, "Merrill Lynch: The Brokerage Giant is Faltering." We read how, "There is no other firm in the world quite like Merrill Lynch & Co. It is the giant of the brokerage industry, from New York to London to Tokyo. In the United States, Merrill's brokerage offices have been known for decades in nearly every hamlet in the land—about 90 percent of all Americans live within 20 miles of a Merrill branch. But the giant is faltering. Its 1984 financial results were dismal. Merrill earned 95 million dollars, compared with 230 million dollars the year before....And Merrill's executive office has been in disarray."[4]

One needs only to turn on the television or pick up a magazine to see that the public education system, without the help

---

[3] *U.S. News & World Report,* May 27, 1985.
[4] *New York Times News Service,* April 7, 1985.

of God, is failing miserably. It is so bad in many areas that 50 percent of those graduating from high school cannot even pick out their own city on a map. In a comedy scene involving Nipsey Russell, the following statements occur: "It's all right to be dumb. But when you cultivate it, it's another story. Free public education everywhere!"

Courts and the legal system have gone far from reality into a realm of complex and weird statutory rules and regulations so that nothing other than the legal system and the police industry is served.

All of this is very distressing, but hardly surprising. "History never repeats itself," said Voltaire; "man always does." Excessive taxation has caused the ultimate failure of many great civilizations—and it is happening right now in the United States of America. "In times of crisis, all governments become oppressive. They tax too heavily," said the great French historian Fernand Braudel. Can there be any doubt that these are times of crisis in the American economy? Or that the government's reaction is to become oppressive and to tax too heavily?

From the very beginning of the history of the income tax in America, there was a fear that the government would abuse its powers. Wise men understood this and fought to prevent the foot-in-the-door, or perhaps we should say the hand-in-the-pocket, that the personal income tax represented. At first, income taxes were collected only to finance wars. Four of the colonies collected taxes based on personal income during the American Revolution. In 1862 an income tax was enacted to help pay Union forces during the Civil War. (President Lincoln was in the five percent bracket and paid an 1863 tax of $1,297.)

The first attempt to collect an income tax during peacetime came in 1894, when congressmen from the South and West pushed through a national income tax law as a substitute for import duties and tariffs. But when the new tax fell heaviest on the affluent Northeastern states, their congressmen responded by taking it before the highest court in the land.

And the U.S. Supreme Court promptly ruled that the personal income tax was unconstitutional!

As Wallace E. Olson reported in an article tracing the history of the income tax:

> The Court held that the framers of the Constitution, having provided Congress with power to levy indirect taxes such as import duties and excise taxes on goods, had declared, "No capitation, or other direct, tax shall be laid, unless in proportion to the census. . . ." In other words, the people of Pennsylvania should not have to pay more direct tax to the federal government than the people of Georgia, except insofar as the Pennsylvanians might be more numerous.[5]

But a crack in the door had been opened. There were too many politicians eagerly waiting for a chance to pry it open all the way. Congress and Presidents Theodore Roosevelt and William Howard Taft agreed that if the Constitution wouldn't allow them to levy an income tax, then the Constitution should be amended. The Sixteenth Amendment, a single sentence declaring that "The Congress shall have power to lay and collect taxes on income, from whatever source derived, without apportionment among the several states, and without regard to any census or enumeration," was drafted by Congress and submitted to the states in 1909. Wyoming became the 37th state to ratify it three-and-a-half years later.

Many of the congressmen favored a flat one percent income tax. Others fought for a graduated rate. Even then, there were some men intelligent enough to realize the danger inherent in a graduated rate of personal income tax. But they were accused of being false prophets making ridiculous,

---

[5]*Wall Street Journal,* October 5, 1973.

unbelievable predictions. They were even branded unpatri-
otic, as reported by Warren E. Olson:

> A fear expressed by a number of opponents was
> that the proposed law, with its low rates, was the
> camel's nose under the tent—that once a tax on
> incomes was enacted, rates would tend to rise.
> Sen. William E. Borah of Idaho was outraged
> by such anxieties and derided a suggestion that
> the rate might eventually climb as high as 20 per-
> cent. Who, he asked, could impose such socialis-
> tic, confiscatory rates? Only Congress. And how
> could Congress—the representatives of the Ameri-
> can people—be so lacking in fairness, justice and
> patriotism?[6]

How indeed!

The personal income tax that became law on October 3,
1913, set a flat rate of one percent on taxable income up
to $20,000. On incomes above that level there was an addi-
tional surtax up to a *maximum* of six percent on income
of more than $500,000 a year. The maximum was soon for-
gotten. The camel had gotten his nose under the tent.

Unjust taxation and oppressive enforcement of the tax
codes, as is now being done in the United States, will be
the contributing factor in the continuing decline and ultimate
destruction of our 200-year-old republic as we know it.

My definition of what has been happening for the last
20 years is that the government agencies have been *Polandiz-
ing* (making like Poland) the U.S. economy. The belief by
Congress and the various presidential administrations that
they can tax the American public, and tax and tax and tax
without limit, has already led to the decline of the American
economic structures.

---

[6]*Ibid.*

As Milton Friedman has observed, "Why don't governments learn? Because governments *never* learn. Only people learn. And the people who learn today may not be the people in charge of economic policy tomorrow."[7]

We must, therefore, prepare ourselves with new methods of economic survival in this new economy that is already well on its way to replacing the old economy.

No doubt you have already been making changes in your own financial affairs in order to avoid being engulfed by an economy that seemed to turn upside down almost overnight. This search for new ways is being forced upon society by its failing institutions. As a whole new economy—the so-called underground economy (I prefer the term free market economy) evolves, the door is opening ever wider for new concepts. My approach is to salvage from the past those concepts which are good and to discard that which is restrictive, while at the same time finding new ways of solving the complex problems of existence in a state of post-industrial revolution. But the ultimate and immediate goal remains the same: tax avoidance and asset preservation.

Tax Avoidance and Asset Preservation

There is nothing dishonest about seeking legal relief from excessive taxation of one's income and assets. In these inflationary times, it has become even more vital for the United States taxpayer—particularly the person falling into the upper-middle income bracket—to protect the resources he or she has built up over a lifetime.

The country's millionaires and billionaires long ago learned the secrets of maintaining as well as enhancing their vast estates and fortunes without seeing them chipped away

---

[7]"Free to Choose: A Personal Statement," publicly televised documentary by Milton Friedman.

by unnecessary taxes. Their methods are *legal*. Unfortunately, the people who are not as rich as they are—traditionally those persons not privy to the secrets of untangling the taxation web—have borne incredible financial burdens from which they see no relief. In a sense, this powerful monopoly on financial planning still exists, but it remains a country club that anyone can join given the proper information.

For instance, what does someone do when he or she is suddenly blessed with the good fortune of earning $150,000 a year? Income taxes alone could be in excess of $70,000. And is there no greater tragedy than for a widow and children to watch helplessly as a comfortable estate virtually crumbles before their eyes due to the onslaught of various government tax collectors?

Fortunately, there are several *legal* weapons with which to fight excessive taxes and controls. More and more taxpayers are seeking and finding relief through what English-speaking people generally call tax havens. The Germans call them tax oases. The French call them fiscal paradises. They all mean the same: Relief. Legal Relief.

Europeans, especially Germans, have long known how to use tax havens, their favored locales being Liechtenstein, Luxembourg and Switzerland. It is part of the life of the average European business person to pursue such endeavors. Sophisticated European business people—people with money or assets—traditionally have some kind of arrangement by which assets are tucked away in case there is another war. It seems that one of history's inclinations is that every 20, 30 or 40 years there is a war. With a trust or a Contractual Company, however, vital assets can be protected in a haven during such a catastrophe.

The information contained in this book is directed toward a legal method of easing taxation. As the esteemed international tax planner Marshall J. Langer has noted:

> Obviously there are some who abuse tax-haven
> facilities, but most foreign tax planning involves

legal tax *avoidance* rather than *illegal* tax evasion. Such tax avoidance is based upon the interpretation of the law rather than the expectation of avoiding law enforcement.[8]

The answer—and a clear conscience—are within your grasp.

Growth of the Underground Economy

"We are in a secular crisis in which politicians are largely powerless to act," says Fernand Braudel, the famous French historian. Braudel offers the following astute observations:

> You see, we are in the midst of a long, historians would say secular, crisis. When a politician says, "We are going to come out of this crisis quickly," the historian wants to laugh. We are going to be in this crisis until the year 2000. Because it is a crisis of structures.
> There is today at the bottom a life of *debrouille* [getting by, managing]—of fraud, of black markets: "I don't pay my taxes, I don't fill in my statement of income." And this is a very considerable layer. This underground economy, which doesn't appear in national income accounts, accounts for perhaps 30 percent of France's national income and 40 percent of Italy's. It is the salvation of the ordinary people who say: "We must go on, we must find a way."[9]

Braudel cites Italy, perplexing to so many Americans. The

[8]*How to Use Foreign Tax Havens* (Practising Law Institute), 1975.
[9]*Forbes,* June 21, 1982.

government has broken down, the big industries are in chaos, terrorists swarm. Yet daily life goes on. By and large, the society resists the crisis. Says Braudel:

> I know an Italian town called Prato, near Florence. Prato does better than resist the crisis. It's a fully prosperous town at the present, full of very small enterprises. Its people work 12, 14, 15 hours a day. They hold two or more jobs. They don't worry too much about respecting the rules. But they're extremely prosperous. That's the way it is: when things fall apart at the top, salvation comes from the bottom.
>
> The [present] crisis is at the top, not at the bottom.
>
> THE UNDERGROUND ECONOMY IS THE SALVATION OF THE ORDINARY PEOPLE.[10]

Presidential candidate Walter Mondale recognized this new economy by stating that he would reduce the national deficits "by taxing the underground economy." He certainly demonstrated his intelligence, or lack of it, with that statement.

Estimates have placed the size of this new economy as high as 30 percent of the total gross national product. I would guess it to be from 23 to 25 percent as great as the official gross national product.

Hegel stated, "Governments frequently get the opposite effect of what they intend." This is certainly the effect of the so-called liberal in the U.S., whose answer to any problem is to pass a complex law and to create an agency to implement the enforcement of the complex act of Congress. This only fixes the problem in concrete, preventing society

---

[10]*Ibid.*

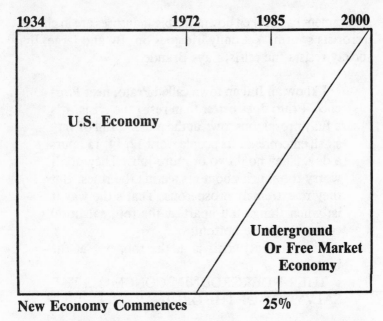

from passing through it. The conservative, who according to Milton Friedman is the true liberal, would leave the matter in the hands of society so that some creative individual or group can find solutions.

"We've become increasingly dependent on government," says Friedman. "We have surrendered power to government. Nobody has taken it from us. It's our doing. The results: monumental government spending, much of it wasted, little of it going to the people whom we would like to see helped. Burdensome taxes, high inflation, a welfare system under which neither those who receive help nor those who pay for it are satisfied. Trying to do good with other people's money simply has not worked."[11]

As Fernand Braudel states, "A wise government sets its people free to develop new solutions. To do otherwise is to prevent society from reforming itself."

---

[11]"Free to Choose: A Personal Statement," publicly televised documentary by Milton Friedman.

Chapter II

The Serendipity or Providential Discovery?

In 1964 I paid $191,000 in federal income taxes and more than $30,000 in state income taxes. Instead of a letter of thanks from the Internal Revenue Service, I received an auditor (IRS Special Agent) named George Berlier, who spent the next several years invading my offices on a daily basis, trying to prove that I had not paid enough.

This man was in my offices virtually every work day, except for two weeks in the spring and two weeks in the fall, year after year. He went through every transaction which had been made by my companies. Finally, after several years Berlier presented a stack of nonsensical documents, more than one foot high, alleging that I owed $1,400,000 in additional taxes for the years 1960 through 1968. This was accomplished by inventing transactions that had never existed, alleging unidentified deposits, disallowing airplane expenses and by saying that I was not entitled to capital gains tax because I was a director in a brokerage firm, thereby attempting to break the corporate barrier and convert my capital gains to ordinary income to be taxed at a much higher rate.

These allegations were not only foolish, but impossible. My total net worth was about $2,000,000 and most of this was unrealized gains. Nearly all of my liquid assets had been used to pay $482,000 in taxes for 1960 through 1964. The balance had gone for attorneys and CPA fees.

It took 10½ years to bring the issue to a conclusion at the appellate level. The appellate conferee stated that George Berlier had done the poorest job of field work in any situation he had seen in his many years with the IRS when complex issues were raised.

The appellate conferee made a proposal to settle the issues for $81,000. His reasoning was that it would cost me that much in accounting and attorneys fees to take the complex issues through tax court. He further stated that the IRS would go to tax court with all four of the issues and that the tax court would give the IRS something. The appellate conferee was the first person with the IRS who made any sense at all.

I had never objected to paying taxes. In fact, I had overpaid since I had not bothered to get receipts for taxis, restaurants, and other tax-deductible items. No effort had been made to reduce my tax liability by sophisticated tax avoidance means, or tax shelters. I had been like a boy scout, straight as an arrow, regarding taxes. I had failed to realize that not only must one work very hard to make money, but also he must try hard and fight hard to keep part of it.

I had founded a brokerage firm, an investment company, and a life insurance company. All had been successful. I had made money. But this was no way to live.

I decided then, after my family had been nearly torn apart, that I would rather shine shoes for a living, in an atmosphere of freedom, than to have all of the money in the United States.

Instead of letting the concepts of control, which were growing stronger, break me spiritually, I did what man has done for hundreds of years when burdened by the yoke of oppressive taxes and controls—I looked for new ways.

* * * * * * *

In 14th century Europe, when taxes imposed by the nobility became more than the working class could bear, there was mass rioting. Tax offices were burned. Tax collectors were assaulted and chased out of town. Some of them even had their throats cut. We have become much too civilized for that. We use accountants and lawyers.

During my own 10½ year siege at the hands of the IRS, I turned for help to Arthur Anderson & Co., one of America's "Big Eight" CPA firms. "Tell me what to do to avoid the repetition of this kind of ordeal!" I implored these noted experts. They knew that out there someplace a means probably existed but they did not know where or how to go about finding the way. They sent me to a fancy law firm in Boston. I spent two days with the lawyers in Boston. They supposed this and they supposed that, but it was obvious to me after two days listening to their supposing (at a fee of $2,500), that they really didn't know with any degree of certainty what I should do. So, I was back where I started—dreading the sharing of office space every day with another auditor from the IRS.

Then, commencing in 1970, I lived in West Germany for two years. While there I became a friend of a prominent Belgian *notar* (an inherited position somewhat similar to that of a recorder and clerk, but one with a higher degree of responsibilities and prestige). I was invited by the *notar* to visit him in Bastogne, Belgium. One afternoon we were discussing Eurodollars and international investments, when he happened to mention that his family had a trust arrangement that went back 400 years. I was fascinated by this and wanted to know more about it. He explained that every 20 years or so one invader or another comes and lives with them in Belgium for a few years. Then they go home. This was his family's way of protecting assets. We spent several hours discussing this ancient trust arrangement, one still very much in force after 400 years. Recognizing my intense interest in the subject, the *notar* said, "Let me make a phone call and arrange a trip down to Luxembourg. We'll meet with some very knowledgeable people and you can learn more about this."

The next day I was in Luxembourg. My Belgian friend opened some important doors for me and, in the process, opened my eyes to effective systems of tax and estate planning that put my head to working rapidly toward finding applications for U.S. citizens. There was no doubt that a tremendous and growing need existed.

After those first introductions, I spent the next two years studying the ways in which business is conducted—and tax avoidance effectively planned—in Western European countries. I thoroughly researched the tax laws in Switzerland, Luxembourg, Liechtenstein and West Germany, among other European countries. During most of that two years I lived in West Germany. What I learned while there convinced me that the failure of the American tax system has made it more and more necessary for United States citizens to arrange their financial affairs in the manner of the West Germans.

Any time you conduct a significant business transaction with a West German businessman, you're likely to be paid with a check written on a Swiss, Luxembourg or Liechtenstein corporation or trust. An estimated 55 percent of the West German business people have corporate or trust arrangements outside the country. West Germany has operated on a thin capital base within its own economy since World War II and that's the reason: as fast as money comes into the country, it goes right back out and into one of the neighboring countries. And what does that money do in another country? It avoids West German taxes. It has found, in other words, a tax haven.

* * * * * * *

Nowhere has legal tax avoidance been practiced as long and with as much sophistication as in the tax haven countries of Europe, mainly in Switzerland, Luxembourg and Liechtenstein. While studying the systems used in these countries was a valuable education for me, I did not want to move either myself or my business to Europe. So I looked for tax havens closer to home.

I spent a year in the Turks and Caicos Islands, several small islands in the Atlantic, just 575 miles from the tip of Florida, that have been a British crown colony for more than 200 years. From that base I began writing and speaking throughout the U.S. about advantages in tax planning to be found in such offshore tax havens, and the significant benefits of offshore trust arrangements for U.S. taxpayers. I was amazed at the response. It was obvious to me that little was known, even among the so-called experts, about offshore trust arrangements for individual American taxpayers. (Even the official IRS agents handbook admits this by stating, "The term 'tax haven' has come to have a connotation that is slightly mysterious. While most taxpayers have heard the term and know that it refers to foreign countries with which some U.S. taxpayers have dealings in order to reduce their federal income tax, little else is known of what these tax havens are and how they operate.")[1] But once I explained how these trusts and contractual companies work, and showed how they are a perfectly *legal* means of tax avoidance, the response was overwhelming. More and more U.S. citizens were asking for my assistance in establishing offshore arrangements as part of their personal tax planning.

Large American corporations have been operating through offshore companies for years. As a senior regional analyst for the IRS in New York, Reuben Tatz, put it, "If I go into any large company and don't find some form of tax haven, I will be very surprised."[2] Indeed, there would not be so many tax havens operating throughout the world if there were not so many large corporations eager to use them for the purpose of legal tax avoidance.

---

[1] Federal Tax Guide Reports in official IRS agents manual.
[2] *U.S. News & World Report,* August 1, 1983.

"The tax-haven industry is prospering as never before," says *U.S. News & World Report*.[3] Edouard Chambost, the noted Paris lawyer who is author of a comprehensive tax-haven guide used by Europeans, said, "The tax-haven industry is alive and prospering and is likely to have a bright future."[4]

If you should have any doubt about the popularity of tax havens among America's largest and most prosperous companies, consider the following documented examples:

- In 1983 the U.S. oil service company, McDermott Inc., a company with $4.8 billion in sales, moved its legal domicile to Panama. According to a report in *Forbes* magazine, a section of the U.S. tax code that forces repatriation of foreign profits in some cases forced the move to an offshore tax haven: "McDermott claims such tax laws prevent it from competing with foreign firms who have more freedom in moving assets and in repatriation of profits. McDermott's prospectus says that if it were to run its business the way it would like to over the next five years, it would have to pay some $220 million in taxes on Subpart F income. Now that it has moved to Panama, that income remains untaxed."[5]

- The *Wall Street Journal* revealed that British financier Sir James Goldsmith's bid to take over Crown Zellerbach Corp. was being funded in part by a foreign private placement of securities of one of his Cayman Islands companies: "Oriental & American Investments Ltd. was created by Sir James last June 12 [1984] in the Cayman Islands to raise funds for possible takeovers of U.S. companies."[6]

---

[3]*U.S. News & World Report*, November 7, 1983.
[4]*Ibid.*
[5]*Forbes*, January 17, 1983.
[6]*Wall Street Journal*, April 11, 1985.

- Texaco Inc., in restructuring debt from its $18.1 billion takeover of Getty Oil Co., entered the Euromarket on several occasions. One example, as reported in the *Wall Street Journal,* was a $200 million issue of 13½ percent notes: "Texaco said the notes were issued by a Netherlands Antilles unit.... This was Texaco's third Euromarket issue recently. Like the others, the notes haven't been registered with the Securities and Exchange Commission and thus couldn't be sold in the U.S."[7]

But these giant corporations, and many others that are far too numerous to name, are wealthy enough to spend hundreds of thousands of dollars to have their foreign trust arrangements properly established and safely administered. It was becoming clear to me that something should be done to make these same legal tax-saving systems available in a way that the individual American taxpayer could understand—and at a price that he could afford.

Since 1977 I have devoted myself to just that: making it possible for the individual American taxpayer to take advantage of the same offshore tax havens that have been used by wealthy Americans and giant corporations for years, but at a price the individual American taxpayer could afford to pay. As *U.S. News & World Report* has observed:

> Now, however, it is the family next door that is taking its turn among the customers of offshore tax havens in various island nations of the Caribbean and the Pacific. Senator William Roth (R-Del.)...says, "The average guy is much more likely to have an account offshore than he was three or four years ago. Such activity has become part of the everyday life of many ordinary Americans."[8]

---

[7] *Wall Street Journal,* July 6, 1984.
[8] *U.S. News & World Report,* August 1, 1983.

Years of study and planning resulted in my discovery of the Contractual Company concept, which became clearly the way to achieve these goals. Was my discovery of this new concept providential or serendipity? The Contractual Company has been blessed from the beginning. It has seemed to work for all purposes. It has proven to be a valuable tool, oftentimes to my astonishment at the ease with which the agonies of probate, death and inheritance tax and capital gains tax could be avoided.

I was also amazed to find that the laws of the land were in harmony with the Contractual Company concept for income tax avoidance and asset protection.

I was prepared to recognize the divine or poetic justice which would result from the Contractual Company concept. Only by being familiar with every business form and document, as well as having suffered the existential crucifixion of the federal government, could I have recognized not only the need but the full significance of the great tool which I had discovered.

Chapter III

Tax Havens Defined

Tax havens are places. They are generally places with little or no taxes. *They are not tax shelters!* Tax havens are commonly confused with the better-known term of tax shelter. When the director of the Internal Revenue Service says publicly that "the sure way to attract an audit is tax shelter, tax shelter, tax shelter," he is talking about a particular business arrangement that relies on accelerated depreciation, deductions for interest payments in excess of the amount invested or actually incurred by the taxpayer, or some other tax write-off in excess of the amount actually spent. These are not the ways in which tax havens are used for effective tax planning and legal tax avoidance.

The IRS agents handbook defines tax havens as "a term that generally connotes any foreign country that has either a very low tax or no tax at all on certain categories of income. However, as the IRS uses the term, it refers to the use of certain foreign countries by U.S. taxpayers in order to avoid federal income tax."[1] Be careful to notice that the IRS agents handbook says tax havens are used by U.S. taxpayers to "avoid" federal income tax. It does not say that tax havens are used to "evade" federal income tax. Although the IRS prefers not to put the effective result into plain print that any taxpayer could understand, this clearly means that tax

---

[1]Federal Tax Guide Reports in official IRS agents manual.

havens can be used by U.S. taxpayers as a legal means to avoid taxes.

Deep within the IRS agents handbook, you will find the IRS grudgingly conceding both the legality and the benefits of tax havens. The handbook states:

> U.S. taxpayers may also use tax havens for tax planning reasons. Some transactions conducted through tax havens have a beneficial tax result for U.S. taxpayers that is completely within the letter of the U.S. tax laws.[2]

Therefore, as long as a U.S. taxpayer is careful to deal only with a tax haven specialist who knows the law and follows it, the taxpayer can avail himself of the substantial benefits found by conducting transactions through a tax haven and remain *"completely within the letter of the U.S. tax laws."*

The average American taxpayer's first response upon being introduced to a system of tax planning with which he is unfamiliar is, "What does the IRS say about this?" So, let's take a detailed look at exactly what the IRS has to say about tax havens and their use in tax planning. The following pages are taken directly from the "Tax Haven Overview" section of the IRS agents manual:

---

[2]*Ibid.*

TAX HAVEN OVERVIEW_____

The Role of Tax Havens in Tax Planning

¶9750 **Introduction.** The term "tax haven" has come to have a connotation that is slightly mysterious. While most taxpayers have heard the term and know that it refers to foreign countries with which some U.S. taxpayers have dealings in order to reduce their federal income tax, little else is known of what these tax havens are and how they operate.

The following material (¶9755 - 9770) presents an overview of overseas tax havens and discusses what they are, their legal and illegal uses and also provides a list of those countries that the IRS considers to be tax havens.

¶9755 **What Are Tax Havens?** While "tax havens" is a term that is heard less often than "tax shelters," it has implications that are very profound for the revenue collecting efforts of the IRS. Generally, the term "tax haven" connotes any foreign country that has either a very low tax or no tax at all on certain categories of income. However, as the IRS uses the term, it refers to the use of certain foreign countries by U.S. taxpayers in order to avoid federal income tax.

• *Characteristics of the Country*

Although there is no formal definition of what a "tax haven" is, the IRS applies the term to certain countries that possess one or more of the following characteristics (.10):

(1) *Low tax rates.* Many of the countries that are considered to be tax havens do impose some income tax. However, all tax havens are alike, according to the IRS, in that they:

(a) impose no income tax on either all or certain categories of income, or

(b) impose a tax whose effective rate is low when compared

to the income tax imposed by the countries whose residents use the tax haven.

Thus, for example, certain countries in the Caribbean (e.g., the Bahamas and the Cayman Islands) do not impose any income or wealth taxes. In the case of these countries, the absence of any income tax is part of a formal policy to attract foreign banking, and other corporate business.

2866   Tax Haven Overview

(2) *Bank and commercial secrecy.* Tax havens generally apply rules of secrecy or confidentiality to business transactions conducted either through or in their countries. This policy of secrecy has its origin in either the common law or in statutory law.

Many tax havens have confirmed or strengthened their common law rules of bank secrecy by statute and/or have added criminal sanctions for breaching these rules. Thus, for example, the Cayman Islands increased the sanctions for violating laws prohibiting the divulging of banking and commercial information without the approval of a Cayman Islands court. This action by the Cayman Islands followed a case in the U.S. in which a U.S. court directed a Cayman Island resident to give testimony concerning bank information before a U.S. grand jury, even though the testimony caused the person to violate the bank secrecy laws of the Cayman Islands and subjected the individual to limited criminal penalties (.20).

(3) *Relative importance of banking.* Banking tends to be more important to the economy of a tax haven than it is to the economy of a nontax haven. Most tax havens follow a policy of encouraging offshore banking business. This is done by distinguishing between resident and nonresident banking activities. Generally, nonresident banking activity does not have reserve requirements, is taxed differently (if at all), and is not subject to foreign exchange or other controls. Banking activities also enjoy the guarantees of secrecy discussed in (2) above.

(4) *Availability of modern communications.* Many of the coun-

tries that the IRS considers to be tax havens have excellent communications facilities, particularly telephone, cable, and telex services linking them to other countries. The use of English as the principal language of the tax haven also increases its attractiveness for U.S. citizens.

(5) *Self promotion.* Most tax haven countries seek financial business and promote themselves as tax havens. Some countries conduct seminars and their governmental officials may collaborate with private individuals in extolling the virtues of the particular country as a haven. In addition, the tax havens facilitate the organization, maintenance and operation of tax haven entities by providing access to competent professional advisors and by adopting flexible, easily utilized, commercial laws.

In and of itself, there is nothing wrong with self promotion considering the potential advantages that a country will obtain by attracting business. However, the IRS takes a dim view of those countries that promote themselves as tax havens by indicating that they have a disdain for the tax laws of other countries.

(6) *Lack of currency controls.* Many tax havens have a dual currency control system that distinguishes between residents and nonresidents and between local currency and foreign currency. As a general rule, residents of the tax havens are subject to currency controls while nonresidents are not. However, nonresidents are normally subject to controls with respect to local currency. These rules concerning a lack of currency control were adopted to facilitate the use of a tax haven by a person wishing to establish an entity that will do business in countries other than the tax haven.

(7) *Tax treaties.* While some tax havens (e.g., Switzerland) maintain an extensive network of tax treaties, many tax havens do not enter into such treaties. However, some tax havens have entered into treaties that, because of the combination of treaty benefits granted by the treaty partner and favorable internal law provisions in the tax haven, make these jurisdictions particularly attractive for certain kinds of transactions. For example, the Netherlands Antilles has an income tax treaty with the United States that provides for an exemption from U.S. tax on certain interest paid by U.S. persons to Netherlands Antilles residents.

Role of Tax Havens in Tax Planning   2867

Merely because a foreign country has one or all of the above characteristics and would, thus, be classified as a tax haven by the IRS, there is nothing *per se* illegal for a U.S. taxpayer to conduct business transactions through a tax haven. It is when these characteristics are abused (i.e., use by U.S. taxpayers to evade their federal income tax obligations) that the term "tax haven" takes on a negative connotation.

.10 "Tax Havens in the Caribbean Basin." Department of the Treasury, January 1984.

.20 *A. R. Field*, CA-5, 76-1 usic ¶9469.

¶9760 **The Legal Uses of Tax Havens.** Tax havens may be used for a variety of perfectly legal business reasons. The following material is an overview of some of the legal reasons that U.S. taxpayers may be inclined to do business through a country that the IRS considers to be a tax haven. It is followed by a discussion of tax planning reasons.

• *Nontax reason*

While the primary motive behind the use of tax havens by U.S. taxpayers is favorable tax considerations, there are nontax reasons that motivate the use of such tax havens. These nontax reasons may be any of the following:

(1) confidentiality of business transactions,

(2) freedom from currency controls imposed by other foreign countries in the area,

(3) freedom from banking controls (e.g., reserve requirements),

(4) higher interest rates on bank deposits,

(5) lower interest rates on loans, and

(6) political stability when compared with other foreign countries in the area (e.g., the risk of expropriation of assets is minimized).

• *Tax planning reasons*

U.S. taxpayers may also use tax havens for tax planning reasons. Some transactions conducted through tax havens have a beneficial tax result for U.S. taxpayers that is completely within the letter of

¶9760   ©1984, Commerce Clearing House, Inc.

the U.S. tax laws. An example of this type of noncontroversial tax planning is the formation of a subsidiary in a tax haven to conduct a shipping business or the formation of a subsidiary in a tax haven to conduct a banking business, where all of the necessary functions are performed by the business entity that operates in the tax haven.

For U.S. taxpayers the use of tax havens alone does not provide a significant tax advantage because the federal government taxes worldwide income. The U.S. tax advantage is generally provided only by the combination of the U.S. system of deferral of taxation of the unremitted earnings of foreign corporations, the U.S. system of foreign tax credits, and the provisions of an applicable tax treaty.

Tax planning can become more aggressive, however. In some instances, the use of tax havens can take advantage of unintended or administrative loopholes. An example of this type of aggressive tax planning includes the use of investment or factoring companies, and some forms of service and construction business being conducted through tax haven entities. A further example of aggressive tax planning is the use, by a multinational corporation, of artificially high transfer pricing to shift income into a tax haven. Basically, the use of tax havens in these aggressive tax planning situations is to shift income and profits into controlled entities located in a tax haven.

Taxpayers that engage in such aggressive tax planning know that, in the event of an IRS examination, a significant adjustment may be made. However, such taxpayers rely on difficulties that the IRS

2868   **Tax Haven Overview**

faces in gathering information from foreign sources and on complications in the examination procedure to avoid or at least delay the payment of federal taxes.

There are provisions in the law designed to prevent tax avoidance through the use of tax havens (see ¶5280-5286). In addition, the IRS is also given the authority to reallocate income between related entities, including U.S. and foreign entities in order to properly reflect income (see ¶4410).

¶9765 **The Illegal Uses of Tax Havens.** The IRS is concerned that countries that are characterized as tax havens are being increasingly used by U.S. taxpayers who wish to escape federal taxation through fraudulent means. The illegal use of tax havens for fraudulent purposes takes many forms. The IRS is aware of the following schemes:

(1) the utilization of sales companies that are structured to appear to reflect dealings only with unrelated parties but that in fact are dealing with related business entities,

(2) the use of foreign corporations that appear to be banks but that are in fact conducting normal commercial operations,

(3) hiding the true beneficial ownership of corporations that operate from tax havens, and

(4) the use of tax havens to hide corporate receipts and corporate slush funds.

In addition, tax havens have been increasingly used by narcotics dealers to "launder" large amounts of cash, and by promoters of phony tax shelters in violation of federal securities and income tax laws.

¶9765   ©1984, Commerce Clearing House, Inc.
                                         000 — 13

Any Place a Tax Haven

It is important to point out that any place can be a tax haven for people from another place. You might be surprised if you asked an expert in international finance to draw up a list of the world's best tax havens and the first country he put at the top of the list was—the United States! As *Time* magazine reported in 1984, "Suddenly America has become the largest and possibly the most alluring tax haven in the world."[3] For decades the U.S. has been an excellent haven

---

[3] *Time,* August 13, 1984.

for nonresident aliens (people who do not reside permanently in the U.S.). It did not happen suddenly, as *Time* reported.

This has happened, purely and simply, because of the failure of our own economy. Recognizing the necessity for attracting capital to finance its gigantic deficits, the 1984 Deficit Reduction Act simply made the U.S. even more attractive. As *Time* revealed, the maneuver was "buried in the fine print of the 751-page 1984 Deficit Reduction Act...a fundamental change in the way the tax code treats foreigners who invest in the U.S. Until then, foreigners who bought American bonds or other financial assets in the U.S. were subject to a 30 percent withholding tax on interest earned. The 1984 Deficit Reduction Act ends the withholding, making the investments tax-free to overseas buyers."[4]

By extending tax concessions to foreign investors, the U.S. is hoping to prop up a deteriorating and dying economy, i.e., the *old* economy that we were speaking about in an earlier chapter. That old economy is already heavily dependent on foreign money. Foreign investments in the U.S. totaled some $86 billion in 1983 alone.[5] At that time foreign investors held a total of $781 billion in U.S. government obligations, real estate, stocks, bonds and other assets.[6] And that was *before* the fine print of the 1984 Deficit Reduction Act made it even more favorable for foreign investors to use America as a tax haven.

Echoing the alarm that many of us have been trying to sound for some time, Federal Reserve Chairman Paul A. Volcker told the Senate Banking Committee:

> We're becoming a debtor country. We're borrowing abroad at the rate of $80 billion to $90 billion. We are directly or indirectly financing that

---

[4]*Ibid.*
[5]*Ibid.*
[6]*Los Angeles Times,* August 17, 1984.

budget deficit from abroad. That's something you
can do for a year or two. I'm not certain how long
you can do it, but you certainly can't do it
forever.[7]

In testimony before the Senate Budget Committee,
Volcker warned that it would be foolish to be lulled into
a false sense of security by an apparently strong U.S. economy that in reality is dangerously weak, at the mercy of foreign investors. "We have severe imbalances in the economy
and we have to begin dealing with them," Volcker said. "We
have been able to reconcile the imbalances at home by drawing savings from abroad. I don't know how long we can
go on this way. There are large imbalances in our economic
performance and points of severe strain here and abroad."[8]
Volcker estimated that foreign investment supplied 23 percent of net savings in the United States in 1984, up from
12 percent the year before.

Too late, the so-called economic experts are diagnosing
the serious illness of our economy, a condition that I believe
to be terminal. Said Brookings Institution economist Barry
P. Bosworth:

Thanks to borrowing from abroad, we're living
way beyond our means. Our children are going
to have to offset that by consuming less and earning more—or else the dollar will lose its value and
earnings of future generations will decline in purchasing power.[9]

And yet the alarming trend continues. The rush to sell
America's enormous debt overseas turned into a virtual

---

[7]*Ibid.*
[8]*Associated Press,* August 20, 1984.
[9]*Los Angeles Times,* August 17, 1984.

stampede after the 1984 Deficit Reduction Act, as revealed
by the *Wall Street Journal:*

> Last month [July, 1984] just after Congress
> abolished a longstanding 30 percent tax on for-
> eigners' interest earnings from U.S. bonds, Mor-
> gan Stanley & Co. slapped fullpage advertisements
> across the pages of two prominent European
> financial newspapers. The message: "Morgan
> Stanley can help institutional investors gain maxi-
> mum benefits from the repeal of the withholding
> tax." The trumpet blare, which was atypical of
> the usually staid New York investment bank,
> alerted investors to a whirlwind of seminars sched-
> uled in eight European cities.[10]

By January, 1985, U.S. companies were borrowing more
in Europe than at home. The *Wall Street Journal* reported:

> U.S. corporations sold more debt securities in
> Europe than in the U.S. last month [January,
> 1985] according to figures compiled by Securities
> Data Co. and *Euromoney* magazine. U.S. issuers
> raised $5.17 billion in debt outside the U.S., com-
> pared with $4.36 billion in the U.S. Last year,
> U.S. issuers raised $21.06 billion in Europe, com-
> pared with $64.34 billion in the U.S., Securities
> Data said.[11]

Time magazine's Board of Economists all agree that the
U.S. is "growing dangerously dependent on foreign capital
to help finance its budget deficit."[12]

---

[10] *Wall Street Journal,* August 31, 1984.
[11] *Wall Street Journal,* February 20, 1985.
[12] *Wall Street Journal,* December 19, 1984.

The United States is now a *net world debtor nation,* owing to other nations of the world more than is owed by those nations to the U.S. Therefore, tax concessions for foreign investors became necessary in order to attract the billions of dollars in foreign capital necessary to pay interest and manage the U.S. national debt.

Unfortunately, the generosity of Congress in reducing taxes for foreigners does not extend to you as an American taxpayer. The point, however, can be made that the American taxpayer should feel no guilt in pursuing a tax haven outside the country since his own government has made the United States a tax haven for nonresident aliens while taxing the average American citizen severely.

Tax Treaties

Tax havens can be divided into several categories, but two of the most basic classifications are the *no-tax* haven and the *low-tax* haven. The no-tax haven is a jurisdiction, political division or country which applies no tax to nonresidents who wish to make use of that jurisdiction. A low-tax haven would be a country with a tax rate lower than the rate in the taxpayer's home country. Low-tax havens are generally havens which have tax treaties with the taxpayer's home country.

There is a very significant difference between tax havens that have a tax treaty with the U.S. and tax havens that do not have such a treaty with the U.S. The difference can be summed up in a word: *privacy*. Privacy cannot be achieved in jurisdictions which have a tax treaty with the U.S. because sharing of information is one of the necessary requirements for entering into such a treaty between two countries. Indeed, by far the largest number of tax treaties the U.S. now has with other countries were negotiated in the decade or so following World War II, when the U.S. was able to get

what it wanted —access to private records of Americans doing business in foreign countries—because European or
British Commonwealth countries were still struggling to raise
themselves from the ruin of war, a struggle in which massive
infusions of American capital were indispensable. Such
countries were in a poor bargaining position when the U.S.
demanded tax treaties that would allow the same invasion
of privacy of Americans doing business in foreign countries
that the IRS wields with such vengeance on Americans at
home.

Therefore, tax haven jurisdictions with no tax treaty with
the U.S., or with any other country, are the preferred tax
havens because of the privacy factor.

And where are tax havens located? Virtually everywhere.
The IRS agents manual lists the following countries as meeting the IRS definition of a tax haven:

30 Tax Haven Countries

Antigua
Austria
Bahamas
Bahrain
Barbados
Belize
Bermuda
British Virgin Islands
Cayman Islands
Costa Rica
Channel Islands
Gibraltar
Grenada
Hong Kong
Ireland
Isle of Man
Liberia
Liechtenstein

Luxembourg
Monaco
Nauru
The Netherlands
The Netherlands Antilles
Vanuatu (formerly New Hebrides)
Panama
Singapore
St. Kitts
St. Vincent
Switzerland
Turks and Caicos Islands

Chapter IV

Tax Havens Throughout the World

A natural place to begin in examining the world's leading tax havens is Continental Europe, where the use of tax haven jurisdictions has long been an accepted practice. Switzerland, Liechtenstein and Luxembourg are Europe's three best tax haven jurisdictions. West Germans in particular have become very wise in how to use these tax havens, which is why it's so common when doing business with a West German to be paid with a check written on a Swiss, Liechtenstein or Luxembourg corporation or trust.

The German people have lost everything three times since 1900 through acts of their own government. This has made them especially astute in protecting themselves against the next contingency. As a result West Germany has operated on a thin capital base since World War II. As capital comes into the country it quickly finds it way out and goes into a Swiss, Liechtenstein or Luxembourg bank in the name of a trust or corporation formed in one of those jurisdictions.

One of my favorite comments on the subject of arranging personal finances was made by a West German businessman who told me, "It is better to live in one country, work in another, and do your business and banking in yet another country."

TAX HAVEN COUNTRIES

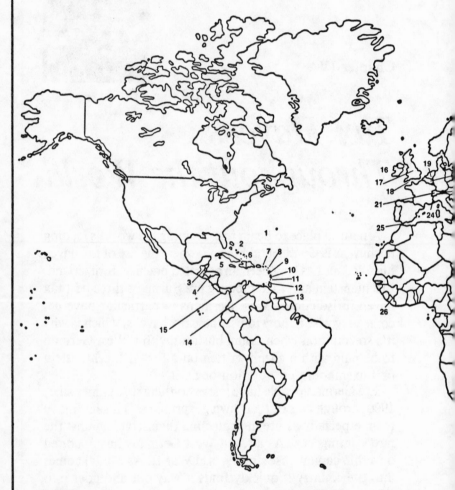

1. Bermuda
2. Bahamas
3. Belize
4. Costa Rica
5. Cayman Islands
6. Turks & Caicos Islands
7. British Virgin Islands
8. St. Kitts
9. Antigua
10. St. Vincent
11. Barbados
12. Grenada
13. Guyana
14. The Netherlands Antilles
15. Panama

16. Ireland
17. Isle of Man
18. Channel Islands
19. The Netherlands
20. Austria
21. Switzerland
22. Luxembourg
23. Liechtenstein
24. Monaco

25. Gibraltar
26. Liberia
27. Bahrain
28. Hong Kong
29. Singapore
30. Nauru
31. Vanuatu (formerly
    New Hebrides)

The concept of Switzerland, Luxembourg and Liechtenstein as tax haven jurisdictions will not go away, even though
French President Francois Mitterand and other leftists might
wish that it would so that the controllers could exercise
greater controls. Europe's tax haven countries are mitigating
factors, deterrents to communism and extreme, if democratic,
socialism. The message is clear: tax havens are places where
individuals can exercise freedom of control over their own
assets and protect them against oppressive governments.

While Switzerland, Luxembourg and Liechtenstein are
excellent tax haven jurisdictions for continental Europeans,
they offer very little for U.S. citizens for the following
reasons:

1. It is difficult to trust your assets to a document written
in another language.

2. Continental European trusts and corporations evolved
under Roman law rather than British common law. While
you can accomplish in essence the same thing, it's much
more difficult for an American to understand the concepts
of Roman law since he has been reared under the principles
of British common law.

3. The demands of conducting important business in
another language are not only tiring but frustrating, and there
is always the understandable concern that one may not fully
understand certain important points, and possibly worry
unduly about it, when documents are written and business
conducted in another language. This is true even if you can
afford the services of an excellent interpreter.

4. A significant disadvantage to the U.S. citizen using a
European tax haven jurisdiction is the limited availability
of assistance from skilled professionals familiar with U.S.
tax laws, U.S. corporate laws and U.S. business rules and
regulations in general.

5. The distance between Europe and the U.S. is an
obvious disadvantage to the average American in using
European tax havens.

The Channel Islands

As we leave continental Europe and cross the English Channel, we come to Great Britain, which happens to be a classic example of how oppressive taxation contributed to the decline of what was once one of the world's greatest empires. Today, Great Britain is a country in economic and social ruin. Excessive taxes helped to dismantle an economy that was the strongest on earth for more than one hundred years.

In the 1970s Britain's tax on all personal income of more than approximately $46,000 reached a staggering 83 percent. An investment income surcharge of 15 percent made the highest tax rate for investment income—98 percent. This was about as close as the government could come to simply taking *everything* a taxpayer had. And what the British government couldn't take while a taxpayer was still alive, it grabbed after he was dead. "Confiscatory death duties are designed to take away anything that remains after payment of income taxes," notes the international tax planner and author Marshall J. Langer.[1]

Naturally, the professed justification for Great Britain's oppressive income taxes was to help the less fortunate. Has it worked? Of course not. As so often happens when government becomes too involved in our lives, a bad situation only became worse. Nobel laureate Milton Friedman, in his exceptional series of commentaries that document how a free market economy benefits everyone far more than a government-controlled economy, had this to say about Great Britain's disastrous policies:

> Ever since the end of World War II, British domestic policy has been dominated by the search

---

[1] *How to Use Foreign Tax Havens* (Practising Law Institute), 1975.

for greater equality. Measure after measure has been adopted, designed to take from the rich and give to the poor. Unfortunately, the results have been very different from those that were intended by the high-minded people who were quite properly offended by the class structure that dominated Britain for centuries.

There have been vast redistributions of wealth, but it is very hard to say that the end result has been a *more equitable* distribution. Instead, new classes of privileged have been created to replace or supplement the old: the bureaucracy, secure in their jobs, protected against inflation both when they work and after they retire; the trade unions, who profess to represent the most downtrodden workers but who in fact consist of the highest-paid laborers in the land, the aristocrats of the labor movement; and the new millionaires, the people who have been most ingenious at finding ways around the rules, the regulations, the laws, who have found ways to avoid paying tax on the income they have acquired, to get their wealth and money overseas beyond the hands of the tax collector.

A vast reshuffling, yes. A greater equality? Hardly.[2]

In fact, the so-called downtrodden workers that Friedman aptly described as "the aristocrats of the labor movement," have suddenly discovered a new way to help themselves: offshore tax havens! As *Business Week* reported:

The most striking example of how high finance

---

[2]"Free to Choose: A Personal Statement," publicly televised documentary by Milton Friedman.

has become a weapon of the working-class struggle is the cat-and-mouse game between the National Union of Mineworkers and the British courts. Weeks before the country's longest and costliest strike was even launched, the NUM quietly converted nearly $11 million of its assets, held largely in government bonds and real estate, into cash. Three days before the strike began on March 12 [1984], the union's leaders set in motion an elaborate scheme to hide their assets offshore.

Since March, the money has followed a circuitous route—passing from England to the Isle of Man, to a bank in Ireland, to European American Bancorp. in New York—before settling in cash and bearer-bond accounts in Luxembourg and Switzerland.[3]

None of this is surprising to anyone familiar with the world of tax havens. To escape the stifling income taxes in their own country, British citizens and companies have long used the Channel Islands as a tax haven. Located in the English Channel, but closer to the coast of France than to England, the Channel Islands became a part of Great Britain in the 14th century. However, they wisely retained sovereignty over their fiscal affairs. There are still no taxes today in the Channel Islands and they meet all the requirements to qualify as an excellent tax haven jurisdiction. British citizens can go down to the Channel Islands, form a trust or corporation, return to London to open stock brokerage accounts or bank accounts, and then invest the funds of their Channel Islands trusts or corporations. In this way they avoid at least some of the excessive taxes in England.

The disadvantages for a U.S. resident in using the Channel Islands as a tax haven are much the same as those recited

---

[3]*Business Week,* December 17, 1984.

earlier in regard to continental Europe: the greater distance involved and the lack of professionals familiar with U.S. tax codes and U.S. business procedures. Although English is the language and British common law is used, the other drawbacks are important enough to prevent the Channel Islands from being a good tax haven jurisdiction for U.S. citizens.

Bermuda

Moving across the Atlantic Ocean we come to Bermuda, a British colony located 580 miles east of the North Carolina coast and approximately 900 miles from New York. Bermuda has traditionally been an excellent tax haven for Wall Street. It is ideal for use by captive insurance companies, for large reinsurance pools, and, under certain circumstances, for large mutual funds as well. The formation of open-end trust, closed-end trust, captive insurance companies and reinsurance pools has been done in Bermuda for many decades.

However, Bermuda has never encouraged the use of its jurisdiction by the average individual for the purpose of tax avoidance. The formation and maintenance of corporations or trusts by an individual American would not only be expensive but also extremely tedious because of the complex set of statutory rules and regulations that must be dealt with in Bermuda. For these reasons, Bermuda fits into the category of what is called a "sophisticated" tax haven, meaning the numerous rules and regulations are too complex for the average person to be able to afford to comply with them. Bermuda, therefore, is not a good tax haven jurisdiction for the individual U.S. citizen.

The Bahamas

Moving south from Bermuda down the Atlantic toward the Caribbean, we reach the Bahamas. The capital of the Bahamas, Nassau, is 238 miles from Miami. Other Bahamian islands are located as close as 78 miles from Miami. The Bahamas is one of the largest and one of the most sophisticated tax havens in the world.

Operating in Nassau are more than 300 large banks, including Chase Manhattan, Bank of America, Barclays, the Royal Bank of Canada, Canadian Imperial Bank, the Bank of Nova Scotia, Citibank, the Bank of Montreal, Lloyds Bank and five different Swiss banks. Nassau is rapidly becoming a world financial center to rival London, traditionally recognized as the world's major financial center. On many days, more money flows through Nassau than through London. While banking secrecy is strictly enforced in Nassau, and information is therefore difficult to obtain, it is estimated that more than a billion dollars per day flows through Nassau.

There are a number of reasons for Nassau's appeal as one of the world's most active tax havens:

• Nassau has an excellent pool of highly trained, skilled technicians from which to draw employees in nearly all areas, from secretarial workers to trust account managers. Not only can you purchase the latest model typewriter or computer in Nassau, but you can employ someone with the skills to operate it and to repair it.

• Nassau's telephone communications system is second to none. Direct dialing to nearly any part of the world is available and service is consistently reliable.

• A number of major airlines service Nassau daily. Airlines

serving Nassau's spacious, modern airport include Bahamasair (the national carrier), Eastern Airlines, Delta, Braniff, Pan American, Air Canada, British Airways and United Airlines. In addition to these major carriers who have regularly scheduled flights into Nassau from Miami and other cities, there are many charter flights. There is also a seaplane service, Chalks International Airlines, which lands less than one mile from downtown Nassau, with several daily flights from Miami and Ft. Lauderdale. Chalks, incidentally, is the world's oldest international airline. The company started in 1919, only 17 years after the first flight by the Wright brothers at Kitty Hawk.

- The Bahamas has a well-defined history of statutory law free from undue restriction.

- There is freedom of currency movement, certainly by non-residents.

- The Bahamas has political and economic stability and a history devoid of violent political uprisings. A colony of Great Britain for 325 years, the Bahamas was granted internal self-government by Great Britain in 1964 and in 1973 became an independent country. It is now the Commonwealth of the Bahamas. The Bahamas constitution and its political system are based on the British system and the country is very much devoted to the capitalistic economic system.

- There are no income taxes, no capital gains taxes and no taxes on interest or dividends in the Bahamas.

- A reasonably high standard of living, combined with an appealing climate and close proximity to the United States, adds to the Bahamas' attractive qualities as a tax haven.

However, the Bahamas, similar to Bermuda, falls into the

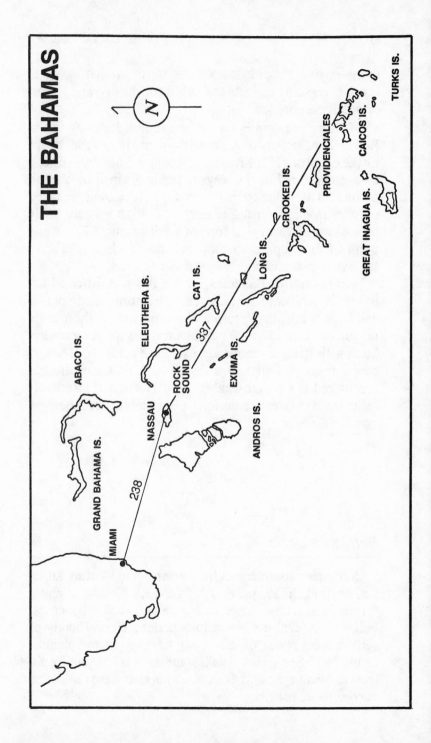

category of a "sophisticated" tax haven, which means it is not necessarily an ideal tax haven for the average person or small corporation.

Offshore banking is the second largest industry in the Bahamas. Many customers are drawn into the Nassau banks by the country's No. 1 industry, tourism. But very little can be accomplished in the way of tax avoidance by a bank account in a foreign country because U.S. citizens are taxed on worldwide income. *Tax evasion* is what you are likely to accomplish through a foreign bank account. The whole point of this book is to show you how to legally achieve tax avoidance and stay clear of *tax evasion*.

Nassau and the Bahamas, as a highly sophisticated tax haven, is excellent for banks, captive insurance companies and large multinational corporations, but not for the average person or corporation. The Bahamas has a strong central bank with stringent monetary exchange controls. It has its own currency. Trusts organized in the Bahamas are not recognized as separate legal entities. The cost of effectively using the Bahamas as a tax haven is prohibitive for the average U.S. citizen.

Belize

Continuing south across the Caribbean to Central America, we find Belize, previously in British Honduras and a former British crown colony. For certain limited purposes, Belize is an ideal tax haven jurisdiction. The difficulty of getting there is one of the strong negative factors against its use by U.S. citizens. The instability in the region (problems in Nicaragua and Guatemala) is also a psychological barrier to its use.

Netherlands Antilles

In this region we also have the Netherlands Antilles, a small group of islands with the capital, Aruba, just 11 miles off the coast of Venezuela. The Netherlands Antilles is an excellent tax haven jurisdiction that has a tax treaty with the U.S. The Netherlands Antilles lobbied hard against the provision of the 1984 Deficit Reduction Act (discussed earlier in Chapter III) which eliminated the 30 percent withholding provision for U.S. investments. Netherlands Antilles argued that the act would ruin its status as a tax haven jurisdiction. But the tax treaty with the United States was of no help to the Netherlands Antilles and it lost the fight in Washington. A severe blow was thus dealt to this ally of the IRS who had entered into a tax treaty with the U.S.

The *Wall Street Journal* reported the following:

> The Netherlands Antilles will begin to lose one of its most lucrative industries. Because U.S. companies can raise capital from overseas more cheaply if they have an Antilles address, about 2,500 of them have set up subsidiaries on the islands...these subsidiaries have issued $40 billion of corporate bonds to overseas investors. European corporations with U.S. tax exposure also have found that Antilles financing units can save them money.[4]

The consequences of the 1984 Deficit Reduction Act could reach far beyond the Netherlands Antilles, thanks to the voracious nature of the Internal Revenue Service. *Forbes* promptly posed this question for the IRS: "Can it void a treaty of the U.S. government?" Reporting on Congress'

---

[4]*Wall Street Journal,* July 6, 1984.

repeal of the 30 percent withholding tax on foreign investments in the U.S., *Forbes* explained:

> And that gave the IRS the opening it had craved
> for years. First it limited the tax-free debt to pub-
> licly traded instruments, leaving issuers of private-
> placement debt out in the cold. Then the Service
> dusted off a hoary revenue ruling and declared
> that it would look to the ultimate recipient of the
> funds in assessing tax on transactions between for-
> eign and U.S. companies.
>
> Gone was the usual "substance test" for deter-
> mining the legitimacy of shell companies. Now,
> if a Swiss company lends funds to an American
> subsidiary by way of the Antilles, the IRS would
> simply ignore our treaty with the Antilles and look
> at the fact that interest payments were going to
> Switzerland. What's more, the IRS wrote the rule
> so that it appears to apply to other countries be-
> sides the Antilles and made it retroactive to—
> forever.[5]

The IRS ploy could, however, backfire. Large companies
are certain to test the new rulings in court, and international
tax authorities have already said the IRS is on shaky ground.
Furthermore, the IRS has seriously damaged the integrity
of the United States government in its treaty relationships
with other nations. *Forbes* reported:

> The other problem, which has our trading
> partners upset, is that the IRS—a government
> agency—has, in effect, voided a treaty of the U.S.
> government. "This unilateral move has hit the
> international community like a bomb," says John

---

[5]*Forbes,* December 3, 1984.

Sanders, a tax attorney with the Dutch firm of Moret Guidde Brinkman. "Can the IRS limit the use of tax treaties whenever it wants to? Can we ever trust a treaty anymore?"[6]

In view of what has happened in the Netherlands Antilles, many other tax haven jurisdictions are certain to be asking themselves that same question: *Can the IRS limit the use of tax treaties whenever it wants to? Can we ever trust a treaty anymore?*

The Netherlands Antilles had attracted large mutual funds to its jurisdiction with the provisions that allowed for a substantially reduced U.S. tax on capital gains and interest and dividends. The mutual funds, as well as several large brokerage firms, had done business out of the Netherlands Antilles. However, it will no longer be necessary to use the Netherlands Antilles since investments made after July 18, 1984, from any offshore jurisdiction will be virtually tax-free.

The Cayman Islands

Another well known tax haven jurisdiction in this part of the world is the Cayman Islands, three small islands in the West Indies northwest of Jamaica in the Caribbean Sea. The Cayman Islands is a British crown colony, one that has been offered independence but has rejected it out of loyalty to the Queen and the Union Jack by citizens who prefer to keep their islands a political colony rather than become an independent country.

About 25 years ago the Cayman Islands set about establishing themselves as a tax haven jurisdiction. All factors were favorable. And its growth in this field has been phenomenal. More than 100 large banks now maintain offices in

---

[6]*Ibid.*

the Caymans and the number of corporations formed there exceeds 20,000. The Cayman Islands, in fact, is rapidly approaching the same level of the Bahamas in becoming a sophisticated tax haven. (Former President Richard Nixon and his banker and friend, Bebe Rebozo, have been reported to make frequent trips to the Cayman Islands. Perhaps, they go only to get a suntan.)

Becoming a sophisticated tax haven, as I have pointed out earlier, also means becoming a more costly place to do business. If the Cayman Islands has not yet reached the full status of a sophisticated tax haven jurisdiction, it certainly is in the process of transition into that category. It has already become more complex, and thus more expensive, to use this jurisdiction as a tax haven. Involved statutory rules regarding the formation of trusts are coming about. And the government wants not only larger fees for the formation of corporations, but larger annual fees as well.

Another development has also had impact on the Cayman Islands as a tax haven jurisdiction. A new treaty with the U.S., supposedly regarding only drug-related cases, has effectively diminished the Cayman Islands' position on bank secrecy. There is frequently expressed fear that the treaty is a foot in the door which will eventually force the door open for further treaties with the U.S.

The bottom line is that the Cayman Islands is a sophisticated tax haven jurisdiction that would not work well for the average U.S. citizen.

There are several other small tax haven jurisdictions throughout the Caribbean area, including some of the newly emerging independent countries, but none of them are worthy of special consideration at this time.

Hong Kong

To complete our global examination of tax haven jurisdictions, we cross the United States (a wonderful tax haven for non-U.S. citizens, as we explained earlier) and go across the Pacific Ocean to Hong Kong. Hong Kong has long been an excellent tax haven jurisdiction. Bank of America, for instance, had not taken title to a major real estate investment, made in the U.S., in a U.S. entity for many decades. Hong Kong corporations were used. When the property was sold, no capital gains tax was required. The money was paid to the Hong Kong corporation, then deposited back into Bank of America to draw interest which would be another tax deduction for the bank. The Lame Duck Tax Act of 1980 ended that practice by removing the exemption from capital gains tax on real estate owned and sold by a nonresident alien. While avoidance of the tax was still possible, it could no longer be done in the same direct manner.

Hong Kong's great distance from the U.S. is an obvious drawback for the average individual. And of course there is another well known problem. In 1997, when the British lease expires, China will effectively take control of Hong Kong, and it's at least doubtful that it will continue to be utilized in the same way that it has been for the 300 years prior to the termination of the lease.

Vanuatu (formerly New Hebrides)

The other notable tax haven jurisdiction in the Pacific is New Hebrides, which recently changed its name to Vanuatu. These islands, located about a thousand miles northeast of Australia in the same general area of the South Pacific as Fiji, are jointly managed by the French and the British. Obviously, it is extremely difficult to get there, effectively precluding their use by the average person or firm as a tax haven jurisdiction. (Despite this remote location, a group of people from Berkeley, California, tried to cause a revolution there and take control of certain New Hebrides islands. What they wanted to do was to expand the services for formation of corporations and trusts and the general use of the New Hebrides jurisdiction for tax avoidance purposes.)

* * * * * * *

Since the beginning of this chapter, we have traveled from Continental Europe to the other side of the globe, crossing several continents and oceans, in examining the world's best known tax haven jurisdictions. Along the way, however, one particular tax haven jurisdiction was purposely bypassed: Turks and Caicos Islands. That is because I believe the Turks and Caicos Islands to be the best tax haven jurisdiction in the world.

The following chapter is thus devoted to the advantages of using the Turks and Caicos Islands as a tax haven jurisdiction for U.S. citizens.

Chapter V

Turks and Caicos Islands: The World's Best Tax Haven

The British colony of Turks and Caicos Islands is geographically identified as part of the Bahamas Chain, located southeast of Nassau, halfway between Miami and Puerto Rico, and separated from the Bahamas by a 30-mile-wide ocean passage. The islands of Turks and Caicos (pronounced Kay-*kus*) lie about 575 miles southeast of Miami.

Turks and Caicos is a separate British crown colony. Associated first with the Bahamas and from 1873 with Jamaica, which is 450 miles to the southwest, Turks and Caicos chose to become a colony of Great Britain in 1962 when Jamaica became an independent country. Commercial routes link Turks and Caicos to the Bahamas and to the United States rather than to Jamaica. Islanders were also reluctant to give up British nationality and passports, since many of them sought work in the Bahamas, in the United States and as seamen. The Turks and Caicos government stressed the population's preference for remaining a British colony.

With a population of approximately 8,000, for many years the Turks and Caicos trade largely consisted of exporting salt and sisal. In the 1980s, however, the Turks and Caicos Islands has aggressively expanded its tourism economy— and declared its intent to become the No. 1 tax haven jurisdiction in the world.

In 1982 the Turks and Caicos Legislature passed a law

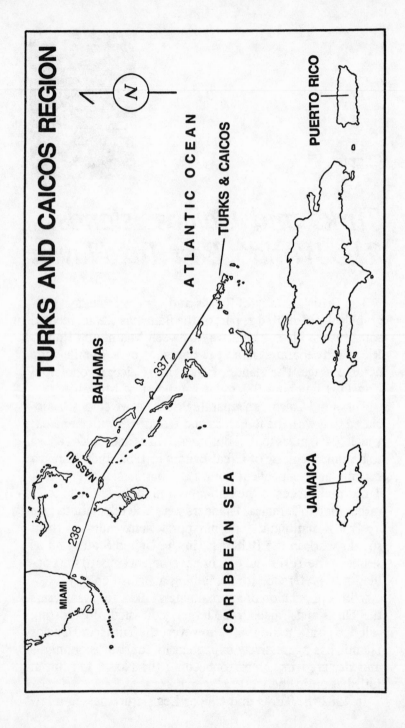

TURKS AND CAICOS REGION

N

ATLANTIC OCEAN

BAHAMAS

TURKS & CAICOS

337

NASSAU

238

MIAMI

CARIBBEAN SEA

PUERTO RICO

JAMAICA

called the Companies Ordinance. Norman Saunders, chief minister of the independent island government which maintains its ties to England as a crown colony, said the purpose of the Companies Ordinance is clear: "To get offshore business here and bring money to the islands."[1] Stafford A. Missick, a former official in the Central Bank of the Bahamas who became Minister of Development and Commerce in the Turks and Caicos Government, cited new legislation that gives Turks and Caicos "the most modern" rules and regulations relative to tax haven laws of any country in the western world and certainly the best among the tax haven jurisdictions found in the Caribbean. Mr. Missick further stated:

> We...established a very effective and a very fruitful dialogue with the local business community...and we sought their advice and encouraged their participation in drawing up a complete legislative program that would establish the Turks and Caicos Islands as a first class tax haven. As of February [1983] we would have completely revised our banking laws. We have put together a team of experts who advise us on all these legal matters. Our efforts, so far, have been tremendously successful.[2]

Indeed, within two years after passage of the Companies Ordinance, there were an estimated 4,200 companies using Turks and Caicos as a tax haven jurisdiction, most of them formed by U.S. firms or individuals. The Turks and Caicos government estimated that the number of companies registered in the islands in 1985 would have grown to some 5,400.

There is little doubt that the Turks and Caicos Islands is now the best tax haven jurisdiction in the world, for all

---

[1] *Chicago Tribune,* February 6, 1985.
[2] *Nassau Guardian,* November 22, 1983.

of the following reasons:

- The use of the jurisdiction for tax avoidance purposes is encouraged by Turks and Caicos law that clearly establishes rules and regulations favorable to the formation of offshore corporations and trusts.

- Great Britain also encourages this tax haven use as a revenue-producing means, thereby enhancing the colony's economic independence.

- There is no tax imposed on any income, capital gains, corporation, dividends, property, estate, inheritance, succession, gift or sales in Turks and Caicos.

- There is no central bank (as there is in the Bahamas, for instance) and no monetary controls of any kind. A tax haven jurisdiction with a central bank and monetary exchange controls means considerably more red tape, and more expense, because of the rules and regulations that must be dealt with each time you or your company conduct a transaction.

- The U.S. dollar is the official currency of Turks and Caicos, thereby eliminating the need to exchange currency and contend with the complications of fluctuations in the value of one country's currency vs. another.

- There is no tax treaty between Turks and Caicos and the United States, or with any other country. This is significant because it means there is no way for the IRS to force information out of Turks and Caicos Islands. If there was a tax treaty with the U.S., then Turks and Caicos would be obligated to turn over information based on that treaty. Even if another country had a tax treaty with Turks and Caicos, that country could come in and demand information on behalf of the U.S. government. The lack of a tax treaty between Turks and Caicos and the United States, or any other country, guarantees the freedom of privacy.

• Turks and Caicos has some of the most severe penalties for violation of privacy laws of any tax haven jurisdiction in the world. Legislation establishing complete privacy in personal financial affairs was adopted as part of the 1979 Confidential Relationships Ordinance. The privacy laws were further strengthened by the 1982 Companies Ordinance. Lawyers or accountants violating Turks and Caicos' strict confidentiality law could be fined $10,000 and sentenced to three years in prison. Corporate professional organizations violating the confidentiality law could be fined $50,000. Turks and Caicos banks are not even allowed to give a credit reference without prior approval from the customer.

• British common law is the law of the land in Turks and Caicos, making it easier for U.S. citizens to understand applications of the law.

• English is the language in Turks and Caicos, making it easier to conduct business and draft official documents.

• The cost of forming companies in Turks and Caicos is moderate and considerably less expensive than in other Atlantic-Caribbean tax haven jurisdictions. Furthermore, while other tax havens, including Bermuda and the Cayman Islands, offer contractual exemption from taxes that might be introduced in the future, Turks and Caicos is the first to not only offer a 20-year guarantee against future taxes but to guarantee immunity from possible fee increases as well.

• There are a number of professionals in Turks and Caicos who are familiar with the U.S. tax code and general business rules and regulations regarding the U.S. (A good example of professional services available is Finbar Dempsey and knowledgeable members of his Turks and Caicos law firm who are well versed in U.S. tax laws and business procedures.) In 1985 there were 13 lawyers and 10 professional accountants practicing on Grand Turk, the seat of government. All are involved in assisting foreign clients in registering and maintaining offshore companies. Only attorneys from British Commonwealth nations are allowed to practice law in Turks and Caicos, which is considered a safeguard against unscrupulous lawyers who represent narcotics dealers and underworld figures. A code of conduct was drafted by Turks and Caicos lawyers for self-regulation of the Companies Ordinance.

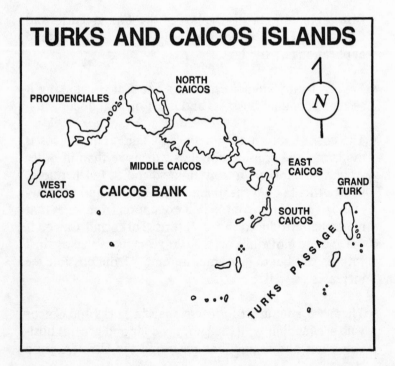

- The distance from the United States to Turks and Caicos is not a prohibitive factor. Cayman Airways has three weekly flights from Miami to Grand Turk, a flight of less than two hours. There are also regularly scheduled flights on Bahamasair from Nassau to Grand Turk. Weekly Club Med charter flights travel direct from New York City to the Club Med resort in Turks and Caicos, a nonstop flight of just three-and-a-half hours. Turks and Caicos National Airways provides daily scheduled air-taxi service to all the inhabited islands, as well as charter services.

- Mail and telephone service between Turks and Caicos and the U.S. are good and steadily improving. The government has been working to install modern telecommunications facilities, including Direct Distance Dialing between Grand Turk and the U.S.

- The security of the British colony of Turks and Caicos has never been threatened because of its long history as a loyal colony of Great Britain. The Falkland Islands invasion by a determined Argentina was successfully repelled by an even more determined Great Britain. At immense cost a small number of British subjects—who happen to hold the same status as the British subjects in Turks and Caicos—were fiercely and successfully defended. This action by the British government was a clear message that its territory and subjects will be protected anywhere in the world.

History of Turks and Caicos Islands

Despite the fact that it is not much more than 500 miles east of Miami, the Turks and Caicos Islands has never been as well known to most Americans as the Bahamas and other neighboring islands in the Atlantic-Caribbean region, such as the Cayman Islands and Jamaica. So perhaps a brief look at Turks and Caicos history would be helpful. It is a fascinating history.

Ironically, it was Grand Turk, and not better known islands in these lovely seas, that historians have documented as the first landfall in the New World reached by Christopher Columbus. This fact is generally ignored by popular history. But modern researchers have established October 12, 1492, as the date that Columbus first sighted the pale limestone cliffs of Grand Turk's eastern coastline before coming ashore on what was then known as Lucayan Island, populated by Lucayan Indians.

The island of San Salvador in the eastern Bahamas was originally recognized as the island where Columbus first landed in the New World, a theory promoted chiefly by Washington Irving. But his reasoning was largely based on

Commemorative stamps celebrate the history of Turks and Caicos Islands and its pride in being a prospering British crown colony.

ancient maps which since have been discredited because of obvious errors in their latitudes. Researchers have since concluded that the honor of being Columbus' first landfall rightly belongs to Grand Turk Island. In 1957, to cite just one of many examples, the Smithsonian Institution sponsored an expedition to investigate conflicting claims on the exact route of Columbus' voyage to the New World. Based on the findings of that expedition, it was concluded that "Columbus landed first at the Turks and Caicos Islands and not at Watling Island [now named San Salvador] in the Bahamas."[3]

After the voyage of discovery by Columbus, the Turks and Caicos Islands existed as a Spanish possession until, in the 17th century, it attracted the attention of French buccaneers. Through the 1500s the islands were a popular port of call for early Spanish mariners who stopped for Turks and Caicos' precious deposits of salt on their way out of the Caribbean from Hispaniola.

The notorious Silver Bank Shoals, a sunken coral reef lying at the southeastern end of Turks and Caicos Islands and close to the northern coast of the Dominican Republic, became known as the graveyard of Spanish galleons. It also became the burial waters for some of the world's most sought after treasures of gold and silver.

Turks and Caicos' unusual Silver Shoals, underwater forests of giant coral that the famous deepsea diver Jacques Cousteau described as "a true garden of marvels, a fairyland of coral," contains more sunken ships per square mile than any other spot on earth.[4] A conservative estimate by historians is that some $600 million in gold, silver and other precious metals and artifacts taken by the Spaniards from the New World were lost in shipwrecks on the Silver Shoals.

---

[3]From the official report to the Smithsonian Institution by explorer Edwin Link, leader of the Columbus Landfall Expedition.
[4]*Turks Islands Landfall,* by H. E. Sadley.

Most of the vast wealth carried by Spanish galleons still lies at the bottom of the sea, buried in limestone encrusted with coral.

Naturally, such wealth has made the Silver Bank one of the world's most famous sites for deepsea divers searching for lost treasures. In 1978, for example, the watery grave of the legendary *Nuestra Senora,* a treasure-laden Spanish galleon that had eluded divers for years, was finally located beneath the Silver Shoals. Several million dollars in gold and silver coins and other rare treasures were retrieved from the galleon that had become embedded in coral on the ocean floor.

A Progressive New Era for Turks and Caicos

Following centuries of domination by the Spanish, and to a lesser extent by the French, Turks and Caicos Islands found new allegiance in the 17th century with Great Britain. It was for many years associated with the Bahamas, also a British crown colony until granted independence in 1973. From 1873 until 1962, Turks and Caicos was associated with Jamaica, the island country 450 miles to the southwest in the Caribbean Sea.

But when it became obvious in 1961 that the short-lived West Indies Federation was likely to disintegrate, Turks and Caicos had to choose between its links to Great Britain and its ties to Jamaica, which was seeking independence. Turks and Caicos wisely chose Great Britain. In 1962 the Turks and Caicos Legislative Assembly expressed its gratitude to the government of Jamaica for past assistance but made it clear that the Turks and Caicos people had expressed an overwhelming preference for remaining a British crown colony.

Under the constitution introduced in 1962, Turks and Caicos Islands established its own elective Legislative Assembly, presided over by an Administrator appointed by the British government. The close ties between Turks and Caicos and Great Britain remain as strong as any in this part of the world, and the British government has continued to furnish solid support to ensure the stability and promote the economic growth of Turks and Caicos.

Turks and Caicos consists of two groups of islands surrounded by continuous coral reef, covering a total area of 166 square miles. The Turks consist of two main islands, Grand Turk and Salt Cay, plus a number of small uninhabited cays. The Caicos group consists of six principal islands: Providenciales, South Caicos, East Caicos, Middle (or Grand) Caicos, and numerous small cays. The Turks islands are separated from the Caicos group by the 22-mile-wide deepwater channel, the Turks Island Passage.

Grand Turk, where Columbus first landed, is the seat of government. It is the center of the rapidly expanding financial trade that is now international in scope. It functions under the most progressive tax haven jurisdiction legislation to be found anywhere in the world.

Grand Turk is seven miles long and two miles wide. It has a resident population of approximately 4,000, nearly half of the island's total population. There are many beautiful bays on the eastern shores of Grand Turk, which is an ideal base for diving and fishing. Grand Turk is lined with beautiful white sandy beaches, as are the other islands.

There are more than 200 miles of sandy beaches throughout the Turks and Caicos Islands. Inside the reefs that surround the islands the calm, crystal-clear waters abound in exotic marine life, making Turks and Caicos one of the world's most spectacular sites for scuba-diving and snorkeling. Offshore fishing grounds are rich with marlin, dolphin, tuna, sailfish and many others, with snapper, grouper and bonefish by the thousands found closer to shore. Lobster and conch are also plentiful.

Temperatures in Turks and Caicos rarely drop below 77 degrees or rise above 83 degrees.

One of the finest reef harbors in the entire Atlantic-Caribbean, the Hawk's Nest anchorage, lies at the south end of Grand Turk. When Christopher Columbus first sighted Hawk's Nest, he described it in his logs as "capable of holding all the fleets of Christendom." This sheltered anchorage is easily entered, with its deep waters providing a safe approach for large steamers.

The Royal Navy frigates of Horatio Nelson once anchored in Hawk's Nest's great natural reef harbor. During the Napoleonic wars the British Admiralty initiated a survey with the intent of constructing a breakwater shelter for naval ships. The resulting plan is now preserved in the British Museum. The King's Agent, Colonel Alexander Murray, reported in 1799 that "the harbour and anchorage called Hawk's Nest was declared by Captain Frazer of His Majesty's Ship *Narcissus,* as well as others of His Majesty's commanders, after accurate survey, far to exceed in safety and depth of water, any other in the Bahamas."[5]

The United States has in the past studied Hawk's Nest as a possible naval base and came close to building a submarine tracking station there during World War II. The Grand Turk harbor was used extensively during the war as anchorage for American Liberty Ships.

Unquestionably, the presence of this excellent natural harbor, and its ability to accommodate at one time dozens of the world's largest ships, will figure prominently in the potential for future economic growth by Turks and Caicos.

Already, the islands' economy has done a remarkable turnaround. With its excellent harbor and good commercial routes to the Bahamas and the United States, the Turks and Caicos economy was for many years based on trade largely consisting of exporting salt and sisal (a strong cordage fiber used in making rope and rugs), along with a small fishing industry. Today, however, Turks and Caicos Islands has

---

[5]*Ibid.*

entered a new era built on a more sophisticated economy. There are impressive signs of its growth throughout the islands:

- More than 1,000 new first-class hotel rooms by the late 1980s has been forecast by Turks and Caicos Minister of Development and Commerce, Stafford A. Missick.[6]

- A new $26 million Club Med resort, called Turkoise, opened in late 1984 on the island of Providenciales (commonly known as Provo). Weekly Club Med charter jet flights offer direct service from JFK Airport in New York City to the Club Med in Turks and Caicos. Nationally syndicated travel columnist, author and broadcaster Stephen Birnbaum described the Turks and Caicos Club Med as one "designed to appeal to the pressured business person. It's certainly the most upscale of the clubs. The new club is very handsome. It's set on a stunning beach, and is a lot closer to most Americans' vision of a first-class Caribbean resort than Club Med has projected before."[7]

- Hyatt Hotels plans to build a 300-room hotel on the island of Providenciales.

- There are now at least eight vessels regularly servicing the route between Turks and Caicos and Miami. In 1980 there were only two.

- The new airport on Providenciales has been completed, featuring a modern new terminal building and a runway that can accommodate jumbo-sized jet aircraft.

---

[6]*Nassau Guardian,* November 22, 1983.
[7]The *Chicago Tribune* Service, in the *Sacramento Bee,* March 3, 1985.

World-class resorts have made the Turks and Caicos Islands a popular vacation destination for American travelers.

- Construction activity in Turks and Caicos in 1982-83 was estimated at $54 million, including residential homes, condominiums and tourist facilities.

- Under the new Companies Ordinance legislation, the number of offshore corporations formed in Turks and Caicos has grown from a few hundred in 1980 to more than 5,000 in 1985.

- Modern telecommunication facilities have been built by the government and are continuing to be expanded and improved.

- Airline service between Turks and Caicos and the United States is regularly being expanded, including a greater choice of flights between Turks and Caicos and the Bahamas.

Never in its history has the future looked brighter for Turks and Caicos. With its year-round warm, sunny weather, spectacular white sandy beaches, beautiful ocean waters that are calm and clear with stunning underwater coral formations for fabulous diving and snorkeling, new first-class resort accommodations and easy access from the United States, these tranquil islands are clearly destined to become the newest "in" spot for Caribbean vacationers.

For our purposes, all of this can be looked on as a nice bonus to go along with what, in my opinion (and I lived in Turks and Caicos for a year), is the most attractive feature of all to be found on the shores of what was the first landfall of Christopher Columbus in the New World:

The best tax haven on earth.

You might say that today's Turks and Caicos Islands is a New World of tax relief, waiting to be discovered by Americans wise enough to chart the right course.

* * * * * * *

In addition to the recognized tax haven jurisdictions
throughout the world which I have discussed, there is
another country that appears destined to emerge as an
important new tax haven jurisdiction: The Co-operative
Republic of Guyana, located southwest of Turks and Caicos
on the coast of South America. In the following chapter,
I will reveal why The Co-operative Republic of Guyana
should now be included as potentially one of the best tax
haven countries.

Chapter VI

The Future Switzerland Of the Americas

The promising natural Switzerland of the Caribbean and the Americas has struggled throughout its history for its identity. With an agreement signed and dated July 4, 1985, between Nassau Life Insurance Company, Ltd. and The Co-operative Republic of Guyana, its identity may be approaching definition and realization.

The Co-operative Republic of Guyana (commonly referred to as Guyana) presents perhaps not only the most complex and diverse set of geographical factors with which its government and people must contend and deal, but also its population is equally diverse from the standpoint of race, religion, and ideology. Thus Guyana's economy is equally complex and diverse.

If one should visit Guyana it would soon be discovered that both Guyana's people and its government are, as its name implies, cooperative.

No place on the face of the earth has God given a nation a more complex set of geographical factors with which to work than those which confront the government of The Co-operative Republic of Guyana.

The coastal plains consist of land below mean sea level. The land was reclaimed from the Atlantic Ocean by great seawalls built by the early Dutch settlers. Therefore, drainage becomes a problem for Guyana, which means "the land of many waters.''

A network of canals are then utilized to alternately flood, then drain, the thousands of square miles of fertile rice and canefields. The canals connect to the numerous large rivers or their tributaries.

The government maintains the canals which supply water to, as well as drain, both state and private lands. The state-owned land is leased to farmers on a cost-and-tenure basis, making the farmer's position regarding the use of the land much the same as private ownership.

Beyond the rice and canefields, along the rivers and on the edge of dense jungles, are situated cattle and dairy farms as well as fruit orchards and vegetable gardens. Then extending to the west and south for tens of thousands of square miles, one finds some of the world's most dense jungles, consisting not only of valuable hardwoods such as greenheart and purpleheart, but also many softer, yet beautiful, and valuable woods. The jungle grows upon land rich in gold, diamonds and aluminum ore (bauxite) deposits.

The jungle rises quickly to elevations believed not to exceed 10,300 feet. While ONC L 27 aircraft navigational charts indicate the highest measured elevations to be in the proximity of 6,000 feet, there is some uncertainty about the exact height of the highest elevations.

Approximately 140 miles southwest of Georgetown, at the end of the narrow Pataro River valley, exists a wondrous, awe-inspiring waterfall known as Kaieteur. A never-ending ribbon of cola-colored water, made brownish-black by the jungle foliage from which it drains, rushes forward to make its drop to the rocks nearly 1,000 feet below.

A landing strip has been built about a quarter-mile from Kaieteur Falls. Upstream from the falls, a mile or so from the airstrip, there is a small settlement of friendly American Indians. A rest house is now being built by the Guyanese government on a ridge about 500 feet from the falls.

Continuing southwest from Kaieteur Falls, after about 30 miles, the dense jungle gives way first to occasional patches of savannas (grasslands), then into a full-fledged strip of scenic savanna along the Rio Maw, which forms the boundary between Brazil and Guyana.

On the Rio Maw there is another small waterfall at a place called Orinduik. A landing strip services a small community 600 feet from the falls. The fertile red soil in this area would provide an excellent area for mechanical farming, dairy herd or cattle grazing.

Southeast of Orinduik there are more mountains, which yield to great savannas which hold the promise of mechanical grain farming and huge cattle operations. However, little is known or recorded about this vast region. The early Dutch explorers described a huge lake where the Indians were said to have thrown their gold. Later expeditions were unable to find the huge lake. It is said that at certain times of the year much of the area is covered with water, making the area appear to be a lake.

Guyana shares more than 600 miles of border on its southern and western sides with South America's largest country, gigantic and friendly Brazil, with which excellent trade relations exist. Brazil, noted for its peaceful nature, has had only one border dispute—never a war. It is said in jest by the Brazilians, about the dispute with Bolivia over the Acree Territory, that 100,000 brave Brazilians were able to withstand the onslaught of 400 invading Bolivians.

It is reported that Brazil has issued a warning to its not-so-friendly neighbor to the north, Venezuela, to keep to its side of the 425-mile border that it shares with Guyana. Guyana is further protected by a defense treaty entered into with Great Britain at the time of its independence. (Guyana was formerly British Guiana, a British protectorate, until it gained independence in 1966.) Mountains, swamps, rivers, and dense jungle afford Guyana protection much the same as Switzerland has historically been protected by its mountain ranges.

One high, steep, flat-topped mountain surrounded by dense jungle, which I observed, would provide an excellent area for precious metal or currency storage.

Guyanese people, consisting of American Indians, Blacks, Whites, East Indians, Arabians, Chinese, and various combinations of all six of the preceding, are not only friendly and cooperative, but hard-working and intelligent. Guyana has some of the most beautiful and charming women to be found anywhere in the world. As a man, I have no such comment to make about Guyanese men. However, my observation has been that Guyanese men are highly intelligent, well-educated, competent, and capable hard workers.

Guyana's government, a republic, consists of 53 elected members of parliament.

The economy has historically been an exploitive one, with its resources being taken out of the country without adequate contribution to its development. Even today gold and diamonds, as well as its foreign currency, are being taken out of the economy. However, solutions are being sought to end these problems. The new tax haven posture, which Guyana hopefully will achieve within the immediate future, may quicken the end of the capital and resource flight.

Guyana as a tax haven has the following advantages:

- Ideally situated on the northern part of South America near the Caribbean, North America and the wealthy South American country of Brazil.
- English is the language.
- British common law is the law of the land (no other South American country can make that claim).
- Guyana will be the largest Caribbean and the only South American tax haven jurisdiction.
- No tax on income earned outside of Guyana.
- No monetary exchange controls for transactions outside of Guyana.
- Bank secrecy laws.
- No known tax treaties.
- Significant size, wealth and prestige to resist pressure and promises from the U.S.

- Knowledgeable professionals (Nassau Life Insurance Company's personnel) to assist in U.S. tax matters and business transactions.
- Pool of trainable workers for support services, typing, etc.

Guyana is a country which has waited patiently, and since its independence been well prepared to reach the threshold of its great potential. Beyond a doubt, progress and prosperity are soon to reach this land which is so rich in natural resources.

Chapter VII

Tax Avoidance is Legal

Before we begin to discuss *how* to avoid taxes, I think it is important to first understand *why* every taxpayer has a right to try to avoid taxes. This means overcoming *taxpayer paranoia,* a common condition provoked by the agents of the IRS. There is a simple truth at the heart of the tax battle——and it is just that, a battle for survival by the American taxpayer—which cannot be repeated too often or too strongly:

Tax avoidance is legal. . . Tax evasion is illegal.

The more you learn about the two subjects, the clearer the line becomes between tax evasion and tax avoidance. The internationally known Paris lawyer Edouard Chambost, an authority on the legal use of tax haven jurisdictions, put the issue into perspective when he said:

> Avoiding unnecessarily high taxes is like looking
> for the best bargain—buying in the cheapest store.
> Evasion, by contrast, means that you are walking
> away without paying your bill.[1]

The reason so many Americans are unaware that such an

---

[1]*U.S. News & World Report,* November 7, 1983.

important distinction even exists is because the IRS has worked very hard to keep them unaware, even to the point of twisting the truth. The IRS, through intimidation, inflammatory news releases and other means of propaganda, wants you to believe that tax avoidance is illegal, if not un-American. However, nothing could be more clear than the fact that tax avoidance is legal and a legitimate right to be fully exercised by every American.

The dividing line between legal tax avoidance and illegal tax evasion was drawn many years ago and the validity of it repeatedly enforced by rulings from the highest courts in the land. For instance, U.S. Supreme Court Justice Felix Frankfurter, a man revered in American history of jurisprudence, could not have been more clear on this point when he wrote:

> As to the astuteness of taxpayers in ordering their affairs as to minimize taxes, we have said that "The very meaning of a line in the law is that you intentionally may go as close to it as you can if you do not pass it (Superior Oil Co. V. Mississippi, 280 US 390, 395-96)." This is so because nobody owes any public duty to pay more than the law demands. Taxes are enforced extractions, not voluntary contributions.[2]

How much clearer can it be? *The very meaning of a line in the law is that you intentionally may go as close to it as you can if you do not pass it.* And, furthermore, *nobody owes any public duty to pay more than the law demands.* In other words, contrary to what the IRS and certain other political elements would have you believe, you are not shirking your duty as an American citizen by doing all that is

---

[2]Justice Felix Frankfurter, In Atlantic Coast Line V. Phillips, 332 US 168, 172-73 (1947).

possible under the law to minimize the amount of taxes you pay. They are, remember, "enforced extractions, not voluntary contributions." And it is, after all, taxes that we are trying to avoid—not the law. The law, incidentally, must say precisely not only what is to be taxed, but also how, how much, when and who is to pay. If a taxpayer can find a legal way to circumvent the tax, the U.S. Supreme Court has said time after time, in strong clear language, the taxpayer has the right to do so.

Read what another U.S. Supreme Court Justice, Learned Hand, said about your patriotic duty to pay taxes:

> Anyone may so arrange his affairs that his taxes shall be as low as possible; he is not bound to choose that pattern which will best pay the treasury. There is not even a patriotic duty to increase one's taxes.[3]

Note that Justice Hand, one of the most famous and respected justices ever to sit on the Supreme Court, used the term "anyone." He does not say Rockefellers, Kennedys, Hunts, or the super-rich. Tax avoidance, while it is also available to and is more commonly utilized by the super-rich, is not strictly their right. The right belongs to *"anyone"* who is willing to exercise that right. In fact, the system rewards those who exercise this right and punishes those who don't. On this you have the word of a federal judge, who wrote in a tax ruling:

> The average citizen, moreover, believes that the government prosecutes only the recalcitrant, uncooperative individual who is unwilling to pay what he owes. Who would believe the ironic truth that the cooperative taxpayer fares much worse than

---

[3]Justice Learned Hand, In Helvering V. Gregory 69 F 2nd, 810 (1934).

the individual who relies upon his constitutional
rights.[4]

During my years of experience in this field, I have found
the above statement to be so true I wish that it could be
engraved in granite and erected as a monument.

IRS agents have an easy time with the naive, naked and
unprotected taxpayer who thinks that the IRS operates with
the same degree of integrity, benevolence, brotherhood,
kindness and understanding as the Boy Scouts of America.
That taxpayer has a rude awakening when, after employing
a CPA, even one of the highly respected (and highly
expensive) "Big Eight" firms, he finds that not only all of
his property but his freedom may be at risk.

Consider the frequent plight of the average American taxpayer. He has read and heard about tax problems faced by
others, but he assumes that those people have problems because they were a little dishonest, or perhaps they did not
employ a good CPA, as he has done. The shocking, startling
facts of life hit home when this taxpayer has his first encoun-
ter with the IRS. The auditor questions every number on
his tax return, demands the backup paperwork for every
minute item and lets the taxpayer know that his honesty and
his respect for the law are in serious question.

The reaction of Mr. Naive Taxpayer is usually the same:
How can this be happening to me? I am Mr. Law-abiding
Nice Guy! Can't this tax man see that? How can this sort
of thing be happening in America?

As someone once said, "It is a wise man who learns from
his own mistakes, but a genius who learns from the mistakes
of others."

It is my belief, based on the experience of many years,
that a taxpayer is much less likely to be audited if he does

---

[4]U.S. V. Dickerson, 413 F20 1111 (1969).

his own tax return, or if he has a small local tax preparer do it. It is further my observation and belief that the IRS, out of courtesy to the large CPA firms, will select a certain number of their clients for audits. The IRS knows from the tax returns not only who can afford to pay more taxes, but also who can afford to pay more taxes *and* huge fees to a large CPA firm.

A secretary for a medium-sized CPA firm, one with five partners, once told me, "The partners are very happy when a wealthy client receives an audit notice." Why shouldn't they be happy? This is the way they make their income. One could not allege that there is an actual conspiracy between the IRS and Certified Public Accountants, but one can easily see an interdependence which forms an alliance or brotherhood with each dependent upon the other for profit and perpetuation.

The web of fear and mystification woven by the IRS is incredibly pervasive. I witnessed a perfect example of this not long ago when I made a detailed presentation before a group of certified tax planners. At the conclusion of my presentation, one middle-aged CPA stood and said, "This plan does not make sense. It does not make sense that the IRS would allow such tax planning." But a younger and obviously much brighter CPA got to his feet and said, "Bill, you surely know by now that it is not a question of whether or not a provision of the tax code makes sense, but rather a question of what does the tax code say, and what does the case law reveal the answer to be." This astute CPA further remarked, "Courts have stated that taxation is not based upon logic or equity."

What is logical or equitable about the fact that the average hard-working American, struggling just to stay even, pays a third or more of his income in taxes while some of the richest individuals and largest, most profitable corporations in the United States pay no tax at all? Every year the same two stories can be found in the nation's newspapers to vividly illustrate the contrast between the average taxpayer and the one who exercises his freedom of tax avoidance. One story annually reports on how many days the average American has to work before he has earned enough just to pay his taxes for that year. The second story reports how many wealthy Americans paid *no taxes at all.*

This, for example, is the story of most taxpayers:

> WASHINGTON (UPI)—The average American will have to work 121 days this year to earn enough money to pay his federal, state and local taxes...the Tax Foundation said. On a daily basis, the typical worker must put in two hours and 40 minutes of an eight-hour day on the job in order to pay all his taxes. The foundation's calculations show that in 1929, the average person worked just 40 days to satisfy his total yearly tax levies.[5]

And this is the story of taxpayers who understand the principle of legal tax avoidance:

> WASHINGTON (AP)—A small group of super-wealthy Americans—299 couples and individuals with incomes totaling $149 million—paid no income tax to the U.S. government in 1982. They claimed enough deductions, credits and investment losses to wipe out their U.S. tax liability....The 299 were among 207,291 couples and individuals with incomes above $200,000 who filed U.S. tax returns for 1982. But since the number of $200,000-plus returns increased sharply from 1959 to 1982, the portion paying no taxes rose from 9 for every 10,000 high earners to more than 14 per 10,000.[6]

---

[5]UPI, April 29, 1983.
[6]Associated Press, January 10, 1985.

Jack Anderson, the nationally syndicated investigative columnist, wrote a column some years ago entitled "The Yearly Tax Ordeal" in which he exposed the results of successful tax avoidance practiced by some of the richest families in America. Anderson reported:

> We have access to secret tax filings by members of our wealthiest families, the Mellons, the Rockefellers, the Hunts and others. Each of the families had had millionaire members, who, from time to time, have paid no income tax at all. And almost all of them regularly pay only a part of the tax their income would require were it not for the use of trusts.
>
> Vice President Nelson Rockefeller, for example, paid no federal income tax several years running. John D. Rockefeller III pays a 10 percent federal tax as a matter of personal principle. Apparently, he can manipulate his tax exemptions to produce whatever return he feels is appropriate. Paul Mellon is able to get away with a negligible income tax as do other members of his fabulously wealthy family. Texas oil billionaire Bunker Hunt has managed to live in luxury without paying any income taxes at all in several years.[7]

I am not singling out these super-rich for criticism. *They have made full use of the tax avoidance laws and that is their Constitutional right.*

Legal tax avoidance by gigantic U.S. corporations is even more revealing. Many of them not only avoid taxes on billions of dollars in profits, but they actually qualify for net tax refunds from the government! Consider this Associated Press report out of Washington:

---

[7]The Jack Anderson Column.

More than half of 250 large, profitable U.S. corporations—including General Electric, Boeing and DuPont—paid no federal income tax bill in at least one of the last three years, a Washington research and lobbying organization reported.

Those 128 firms earned profits of $56.7 billion from U.S. operations in the 1981-1983 period. In 1983 alone, the report states, 130 of the corporations that were surveyed earned profits totaling $45 billion but paid less tax than the 12 percent paid by the average family.

Many of the companies actually paid less than no tax—legally taking advantage of the federal tax system to gain refunds totaling $5.7 billion, according to a report by Citizens for Tax Justice.

GE earned $6.5 billion in pretax domestic profits over the three years, paid not one cent of federal income taxes and claimed tax refunds of $283 million.

Eighty-eight percent of the 250 companies were listed by *Forbes* magazine as among the 500 most profitable in 1983. Each made a profit in each of the last three years. Citizens for Tax Justice said that in addition to General Electric, six firms— Boeing, Dow Chemical, Tenneco, Santa Fe Southern Pacific, Weyerhaeuser and DuPont—each received more than $100 million in net tax refunds over the three years. Seventeen companies paid zero or less tax in each of the three years.

The 250 companies that responded to the survey earned $102.2 billion in profits last year and paid 14.6 percent of that in federal income taxes.[8]

Let us take another look at what yet another U.S.

---

[8]Associated Press, October 6, 1984.

Supreme Court Justice, George Sutherland, said about the legality of tax avoidance:

> The legal right of a taxpayer to decrease the amount of what otherwise would be his taxes, or altogether avoid them, by means which the law permits cannot be doubted.[9]

Notice that Justice Sutherland stated this as a "legal right," not a "privilege," something that might or might not be granted. Also note further that while Justice Learned Hand wrote in counterpart to that case, Helvering vs. Gregory, that a taxpayer can make his taxes as low as possible, Justice Sutherland went a step further and said that not only can a taxpayer decrease his taxes, but he may *altogether avoid them*. It is his "legal right."

And notice how strong Justice Sutherland is on this point of the right to avoid taxes: it *"cannot be doubted."* Why should we doubt it? The Supreme Court says it's so. That makes it the law of the land. Yet many do doubt it. They rely on the belief that since they are nice, honest, hard-working, patriotic, tax-paying Americans, there can be no problem with the IRS.

How wrong they are! As that federal judge observed, who would believe the ironic truth that the cooperative taxpayer fares much worse than the individual who relies upon his constitutional rights. You should believe it because you will never save one nickel on taxes, or in many instances even be able to keep that portion of your earnings which should rightfully be yours, unless you try.

---

[9]Justice George Sutherland, In Gregory V. Helvering 239 US 465, 469 (1934).

Chapter VIII

The Corporation

The system which I utilize in assisting the individual American taxpayer achieve legal tax avoidance through use of an offshore tax haven jurisdiction, in this instance the Turks and Caicos Islands, is built on the creation and effective operation of the Contractual Company. However, to better understand the methods used within this system, we need to first understand what a corporation is in order to understand the workings of a Contractual Company.

A corporation is a separate, distinct, legal, judicial or artificial entity formed by a set of statutory rules, regulations or laws adopted by the legislature or lawmaking authority of a political division, legal jurisdiction or country with sovereignty to make such laws and to grant such privilege. Since corporations are formed by a set of statutes describing how to form such an entity, they are frequently referred to as statutory entities.

While corporations may be formed only for a single, specific purpose, they are generally formed with broad powers and essentially have many of the rights and privileges of a live, breathing person. However, U.S. courts have said consistently that the Bill of Rights of the Constitution does not apply to artificial entities whose privilege to exist is granted by a political jurisdiction. Therefore, corporations have no constitutional protection against unlawful search and seizure. The whole corporation can be taken into receivership at the whim of a federal or state judge. The assets of the corporation can be placed in the hands of a court-appointed receiver. That receiver can do just about as he chooses, with the sanction or blessing of the court. The Bill of Rights of the Constitution applies only to live, breathing people.

The U.S. Supreme Court ruled on this question of the individual's rights vs. the corporation's rights in the landmark decision, Hale vs. Henckle. The court held:

> Conceding that the witness was an officer of the corporation under investigation, and that he was entitled to assert the rights of the corporation with respect to the production of its books and papers, we are of the opinion that there is a clear distinction in this particular between an individual and a corporation, and that the latter has no right to refuse to submit its books and papers for an examination at the suit of the State. The individual may stand upon his constitutional rights as a citizen. He is entitled to carry on his private business in his own way. His power to contract is unlimited. He owes no duty to the State or to his neighbors to divulge his business, or to open his doors to an investigation, so far as it may tend to incriminate him. He owes no such duty to the State, since he receives nothing therefrom, beyond the protection of his life and property. His rights are such as existed by the law of the land long antecedent to the organization of the State, and can only be taken from him by due process of law, and in accordance with the Constitution. Among his rights are a refusal to incriminate himself, and the immunity of himself and his property from arrest or seizure except under a warrant of the law. He owes nothing to the public so long as he does not trespass upon their rights.

Upon the other hand, the corporation is a creature of the State. It is presumed to be incorporated for the benefit of the public. It receives certain special privileges and franchises, and holds them subject to the laws of the State and the limitations of its charter. Its powers are limited by law. It can make no contract not authorized by its charter. Its rights to act as a corporation are only preserved to it so long as it obeys the laws of its creation. There is a reserved right in the legislature to investigate its contracts and find out whether it has exceeded its powers. It would be a strange anomaly to hold that a State, having chartered a corporation to make use of certain franchises, could not in the exercise of its sovereignty inquire how these franchises had been employed, and whether they had been abused, and demand the production of the corporate books and papers for that purpose. The defense amounts to this: That an officer of a corporation, which is charged with a criminal violation of the statute, may plead the criminality of such corporation as a refusal to produce its books. To state this proposition is to answer it. While an individual may lawfully refuse to answer incriminating questions unless protected by an immunity statute, it does not follow that a corporation, vested with special privileges and franchises, may refuse to show its hand when charged with an abuse of such privileges.[1]

A typical corporate charter would include:

• The right to sue and to be sued.
• The right to own property, both real and intangible, of

---

[1]Hale vs. Henckle, 201 US at 74, 1905.

any kind, shape, form or description.
• The right to engage in any lawful business.

Since the corporation cannot think for itself, someone must do that for it. Thinking and decision-making for the corporation are therefore done by a board of directors consisting of not less than one nor more than a specified number set forth in the corporate charter.

The decisions of the board are then carried out by officers who are elected by the board of directors. The officers then conduct the business of the corporation: buying, selling, hiring, firing and performing all of the acts on behalf of the corporation in compliance with the decisions of the board of directors and the bylaws of the corporation.

The officers are not, while in the employment of the corporation, acting for themselves. They are acting for the corporation.

When the corporation is formed, it has no money or assets at all, except its own shares which it must sell or exchange in order to acquire money or assets. The purchasers of the shares become the shareholders. The shareholders then have the right to elect the board of directors at shareholder meetings, with usually one vote for each share held. The shareholder meetings are usually held annually.

Advantages of Forming a Corporation

A prime advantage of the corporation is limited liability to the live, breathing people who own the corporation and work for it.

The corporation shareholders have limited liability in the sense that all shares must be fully paid and nonaccessible when issued and the shareholders can only be held responsible for the amount of money they have paid or agreed to pay for the shares.

Another advantage is centralized management. The board of directors is granted decision-making authority and the authority to select officers to manage the business of the company. Information flows to and from the board. Hopefully, the input of information leads to the right decisions being made and a successful business.

Continuity of existence also is achieved with the corporation. An individual can die at any time; however, a corporation's charter states the length of the entity's life. While the charter could be for a ten-, fifty- or hundred-year period, most charters are issued *forever*. Continued existence is usually contingent upon payment of fees to the state, country or political division which granted the corporation its charter and thus made possible its existence. In many jurisdictions, an annual report showing the names of the officers and directors of the corporation is required by law.

Flexibility is another attribute of the corporation. If the officers do not perform well, they can be replaced by the board of directors. If the board does not perform well, it can be replaced at a special or an annual shareholders meeting.

Should the main business of the corporation turn sour, it can select and enter into another business.

The corporation can acquire and own other corporations engaged in any kind of lawful business.

If all of the share capital is used up in mergers, exchanges, splits, dividends, etc., more shares can be created at a shareholders meeting by the shareholders. Thus the growth of the corporation because of its flexibility can be unlimited.

The corporation has been a great device for making large capital accumulation for the financing of industry, housing and distribution of goods and services. There is nothing inherently good or evil about a corporation. It is simply a formalized tool, established and regulated by law, by which mankind can better provide for its needs and desires.

But the U.S. tax code has effectively negated the use of the offshore corporation as a tax planning tool. There is a "big thick" section in the "big thick tax code" regarding controlled foreign corporations. Basically, if a U.S. taxpayer owns 10 percent or more of the outstanding shares of the corporation, it is considered to be a controlled foreign corporation with severe tax penalties.

Chapter IX

The Trust

The term *trust* is a concept that is grossly misunderstood. Promoters too often make a trust sound like some kind of mystical or magical set of documents. (The more mystical lawyers can make something seem, the higher fees they can charge.)

Trusts are frequently created by people without their knowledge that a trust has been created. Nearly everyone has at sometime or other acted as a trustee, a trustor or the beneficiary of a trust. The kind of trust we are talking about here is a *verbal* trust.

If you have ever handed a sum of money to another person with which he or she was to pay a bill or fulfill any specified purpose, you formed a verbal trust. You were the *trustor,* the person to whom you turned over the money was the *trustee,* and the final recipient of the money was the *beneficiary* of that trust. Trusts have been simply defined as property held by one for the benefit of another.

If, in the above example, you had said to the recipient of the funds, "If I come back and ask for the money before you turn it over to the beneficiary, you must give it back to me," you would have formed a *revocable* trust.

On the other hand, if you had said to the recipient of the funds, "Regardless of the circumstance, if I come back to you and ask for the money, do not give it to me. Make sure the money goes only to the beneficiary," then you have formed an *irrevocable* trust.

As you can easily see from these examples, mom and dad have probably formed many trusts with you—both revocable and irrevocable.

I can hear mom saying, "No, you cannot have that money. You are saving it for college." She is enforcing an irrevocable trust.

Such verbal trusts are legal. As a matter of fact, the California Probate Form contains the following questions:

"Did decedent place property in trust during his or her lifetime?"

"If the answer to the above question is yes, was the trust written or verbal?"

The problem with a verbal trust is one of evidence. How can you prove that you gave the money or the property to John with instructions that it be passed on to Jane? You could go into court and say, "I gave money to John to pass on to Jane." But John could say, "No, he did not give me any money for Jane." Or, what if John dies before he gives the money to Jane? It would be difficult to distinguish between your money that was given to John and his own money. It would therefore be extremely difficult for you to make a claim against John's estate, based solely on the contention that you gave John money and verbal instructions to pass it on to Jane.

On the other hand, if John had written something down, even if only on the back of an envelope or on any scrap of paper, to the effect that, "I, John Jones, acknowledge receipt of $1,000 from James Smith on this 15th day of May 1985. Said funds are to be turned over to Jane Smith when I next see her," you would have evidence. You and John would have made a written trust, with Jane as beneficiary.

Trusts, of course, are generally much more complex than the simple trusts described above. However, the principle is the same—something turned over to someone either for his own benefit or the benefit of a third party.

The Uses for a Trust

Trusts can be written in as many different ways as a contract can be written to achieve almost any lawful purpose.

The most common uses for a trust are:

- Achieving limited liability for a portion of one's wealth.
- Setting aside money for retirement.
- Passing on one's estate to the next generation.
- Providing special benefits for family members, such as education, planned income, housing, health care, other personal needs.
- For tax deferral purposes.
- For conducting business (mutual funds).

Trusts are contracts. The freedom or right to contract is well protected in the Constitution of the United States of America.

Trust promoters are fond of making high-minded statements to the effect that their trust *cannot be broken*. This sounds impressive, but it really isn't saying very much.

Their particular set of documents could be broken or invalidated for the same reasons any contract could be invalidated, namely, insanity or mental incompetence on the part of the maker of the trust, as well as fraud or coercion used in making the trust.

The Grantor Trust

The IRS tax code has a big, thick section on trusts. The type of trust covered by this section is the one called a Grantor Trust. In a Grantor Trust, the person owning property exchanges the property for a certificate of beneficial interest and appoints himself or someone else to act as trustee.

The receipt of tax benefits through the Grantor Trust is

often dependent upon whether the trust is revocable or irrevocable. Such Grantor Trusts can be of benefit if gifts are to be made to relatives from the trusts in compliance with the gift tax act.

The Foreign Trust

The U.S. tax code defines a foreign trust as an "estate or trust...the income of which, from sources without the United States which is not effectively connected with the conduct of a trade or business within the United States, is not includible in gross income under Subtitle A."[1] A U.S. citizen is fully taxable on the earnings of a foreign bank account, but taxes can be legally avoided through proper use of an offshore or foreign trust arrangement. These trusts are legally termed a "foreign *situs* trust," *situs* meaning a fixed site.

International tax planners have long recognized the benefits of placing assets in a foreign trust. Attorneys Quentin L. Breen and Douglas H. Wolf, authors of the esteemed publication *United States Law and Practice,* take note of this:

> For the United States taxpayer the foreign *situs* trust offers a remarkable opportunity for long-range tax deferral and the management of an investment portfolio. The foreign *situs* trust permits the United States investor to achieve parity with the nonresident alien by expatriating his capital. Properly structured, a foreign *situs* trust qualifies as a "nonresident alien individual" and achieves "most favored investor" status for the

---

[1] Internal Revenue Code, 7701 (a) (31).

United States citizen investing either at home or abroad.[2]

The foreign trust must comply with the following rules and regulations of the U.S. tax code in order to qualify as a separate taxable entity and thus enjoy the considerable tax savings as a nonresident alien:

1. It must constitute a trust under both the laws of the United States and the foreign jurisdiction in which the trust is formed.

2. The trust must be created outside the United States.

3. The trust must be subject to the laws of the foreign jurisdiction in which it is created.

4. The trustee cannot be a resident of the United States.

The Origin and History of the Pure Trust and Contractual Company

The pure trust, from which the Contractual Company evolved, is an entity not new to the world, going back as far as 800 years A.D. during the Roman Empire. It became the preferred method of establishing equity of ownership and management in the Middle Ages on the European continent. Medieval clergy used trusts as a way of holding monasteries so that monks could use property without violating their vows of poverty. When the American colonies adopted the common law of England, English principles of equity were also adopted. In fact, the first pure trust of record in America was recorded in 1765 — 23 years before the adoption of the Constitution—for Governor Robert Morris of

---

[2]*United States Law and Practice,* by Quintin L. Breen, J.D. and Douglas H. Wolf, J.D. of Breen, Kantor and Wolf Law Corporation.

the colony of Virginia who was later a prominent financier of the American Revolution.

English pure trust history is well worth examining. These early trusts, mothered by necessity as so many inventions have been, were modeled after the ancient German legal receiver called the "salman." He was a person to whom land was transferred in order that he might make a conveyance according to the former owner's wishes. Although this might seem a devious and inefficient way of transferring property, a review of the conditions in medieval times should show the reasons for this procedure.

In England, many burdens and conditions fell upon the holder of legal title to real estate. For example, the lord of the land was entitled to relief or money payments when the land was passed to an heir of full age. The lord was given the right to claim wardship fees when the son of the former owner was a minor. The lord was also entitled to aid or tax money to pay for the marriage of the lord's daughter or the knighting of the lord's eldest son. In addition, the owner of the land was usually prohibited from selling the land or dividing it among his children or grandchildren. If the owner of the land was convicted of a crime, he forfeited all he owned to the lord or king, thereby leaving his family impoverished. These were the major restrictions. There were nearly 100 other taxes and limitations on the owners of land.

To avoid these restrictions under the law, the trust—a creation of the Court of Chancery in England—was originally developed. It was designed to avoid the application of rigid laws relating to the succession of property by allowing the trustor (or settler) to vest legal title in a trustee on behalf of a wife, son, daughter, or other person as beneficiary. It had many advantages, including that it could be kept secret. The king did not have to know of the transfer of property to trustees, but by law the taxes and other limitations could be ignored.

The attractions of the ancient trust are obvious. It enabled a person to enjoy privacy under a system that usually demanded disclosure. The trust enabled a person to avoid some of the burdens of special taxes. The trust allowed individuals to "sell" land and to pass it to those they wished.

Over the years, many versions of pure trusts were developed, but their basic goals remained to preserve English family estates and to keep them out of the hands of the king. Obviously, while the ancient trust has evolved into a full body of rules governing the relationship between parties, the same goals are desirable today. The present tax system has imposed certain burdens and restrictions on the citizens of our country that are comparable to the burdens and restrictions that limited the citizens of ancient England, in the sense that property is not necessarily safe from judgments, liens or tax authorities. For instance, not only does the government have a complete record of your assets from your tax returns, but it can go in and get any information it wants from your bank account and by subpoena *dueces tecum* take all of the records of a U.S. trust or corporation which under the laws have no civil rights.

Fortunately, a descendant of the pure trust is alive and well. Unfortunately, the knowledge of its existence seems only to be in the sharp minds and accounting hands of the nation's rich.

For instance, prominent financier William Waldorf Astor created a $50 million trust estate by a conveyance to trustees, recorded in New York in 1919. By doing this, he saved his heirs several million dollars which would have gone for inheritance taxes had the estate been distributed by the court instead of trustees.

The Rockefeller family has used various kinds of trusts as a means of minimizing inheritance taxes and maximizing privacy. Before his death in 1937, John D. Rockefeller tucked much of his fortune into about 70 trusts for his descendants. The vast web of individual group funds represented assets of considerably more than $1 billion. Then the late Nelson A. Rockefeller and his generation are believed to have reduced their personal holdings by the creation of still more trusts for their grandchildren and great grandchildren. According to one source, there are well over 100 and perhaps even 250 individual Rockefeller trusts by now. Many of these trusts are known to be pure trusts to place funds beyond reach of probate and inheritance tax laws.

In addition, the late Texas oil billionaire H. L. Hunt is reported to have paid $75,000 to establish the first Hunt family pure trust. His attorneys then copied the first trust indenture and formed at least 25 additional trusts.

Beware the Unscrupulous Offshore Trust Promoters

Few subjects have been so misunderstood, or a concept so difficult not only for the average person but also for lawyers and accountants to understand, as are trusts in general and offshore trusts, or foreign trusts, in particular. Both the domestic trust and the offshore trust have been so enveloped by mystery and misunderstanding that the suede shoe promoters, as well as the not-so-slick country bumpkins, can fleece innocent American taxpayers and unsophisticated business people out of large sums of money by stealing and copying documents about which the promoters know little or nothing. This is done by espousing the mystical and magical benefits of the set of documents (trusts) that they are touting.

I have one word of advice for you in dealing with such promoters: *beware!*

Just owning the set of documents without the legal and practical expertise of a qualified organization to administer and defend the trust can cause many more problems than they can ever hope to resolve. Let me give you some examples of which I am personally aware.

One trust promoter from Arizona sold an offshore trust to a Northern California resident for $5,000. The trust purchaser's name spelled backward was listed on the documents as the trustee. Real property was transferred to the so-called trust. So far, so good. There was no problem. But after the transfer, the property was listed and sold. *Then* there was a problem. A big problem. How could a nonexistent trustee execute the deed and obtain title insurance? And the title officer, being somewhat more than a common fool, noticed immediately after the document was presented for his inspection that the name of the trustee was in fact the name of the trustor (the person for whom the trust was created) spelled backward. Naturally, there were serious legal repercussions for this person who had become party to an illegal offshore trust created by an unscrupulous trust promoter.

The stupidity, let alone the illegality, of that operation might sound unbelievable, but it's absolutely true. And here are more true stories that seem just as ridiculous.

A disbarred attorney (now in jail) obtained informational material and a set of trust documents from Nassau Life Insurance Company, Ltd. He proceeded to remove the Company name and the name of the Company president from the material and the documents. He then started selling offshore trusts using these documents! The problem was that he was having the documents which he sold signed before a U.S. notary public. Did that form a foreign trust? It certainly did not! The documents for which purchasers had paid thousands of dollars were absolutely worthless. The individual involved even had the audacity to charge $10 for each question he answered for the client after the purchase of these worthless, fraudulent documents.

Some people don't need outsiders' help in making fools of themselves—they're quite capable of doing it on their own. For example, there was a group from Oregon that bought trusts from Nassau Life Insurance Company, Ltd. They attended a day or so of what was actually a seven-day seminar on offshore trusts and then became self-proclaimed experts in this field. The documents of Nassau Life Insurance Company, Ltd. were copied verbatum and the group began marketing the documents at a supposed bargain price. The signature on the documents was a large spiral, no more than a giant scrawl, that was not legible to anyone. Nonetheless, the documents were notarized and executed by nonresidents of the Turks and Caicos Islands.

These trusts were marketed as *secret* trusts by the ill-informed, self-proclaimed experts. What in the world could anyone do with a secret trust? Can he put property in it? Can it have a bank account? Can it hold or buy and sell property, or anything else, in its own name? If it could, and it did buy and sell, it would not be secret, would it? Bargain trusts? Not at any price!

Written documents, although they do not necessarily need to be lengthy or complicated, are absolutely essential to the legal formation and operation of any effective trust, including the offshore trust. These documents, proof that the trust exists, are required by recorders, public officials, banks, title insurance firms and stock brokerage firms in order to transact business. A verbal trust would be of as much value as a secret trust in these matters. The notion of a secret trust which will never come to light is foolish on its face. If it is a secret, why have one? What would one do with it?

The set of documents which form the trust, establishing it as a separate, distinct legal entity, may cost only a few dollars to reproduce by those who purchase and copy—or steal and copy—the documents for the purpose of selling them to individuals seeking asset protection, estate preservation or tax reduction planning. But in truth you are not buying much more than pieces of paper.

The important question is, *What services go with the set of documents which you purchase?*

Does the promoter of the trust have the financial means to back up his claims?

Does the promoter of the trust have proper legal opinions pertaining specifically to his set of documents?

Does the promoter of the trust have offices and representatives in the jurisdictions in which the trusts are being formed?

Is the promoter of the trust willing and capable of defending his claims in courts—all the way to the U.S. Supreme Court if necessary?

Are competent, well-trained personnel readily available by phone to answer all questions regarding any kind of transactions involving the trust?

Is assistance available for filling out forms for opening accounts or dealing with assessors and tax collectors?

And, the most important question of all: *Can the trustee be trusted to the same extent that you trust the people or institutions that you normally trust to handle your money or other assets?*

In critical economic times throughout recent history, trusts have served mankind well. As economic conditions become severe, governments always become tyrannical. The individual must therefore seek protection of his property or else lose it to those with the government power to take it because the government has passed laws giving themselves that power. It will be legally taken, just as the accused must be given a fair trial before his hanging. The legal means naturally justifies the act of hanging the accused, or the taking of a person's property. But in any event, the hanged man is dead—and the property is long gone from its rightful owner.

In order to have a worthwhile offshore trust, one into which you can place your assets with a great degree of confidence, the trust must be able to withstand the scrutiny of the IRS, the courts or any other authority. *It must and should be open and aboveboard.*

Chapter X

The Contractual Company

The Contractual Company, which will be explained in a step-by-step process in this chapter, is in fact a new approach to an old way of conducting business, wherein the following desirable objectives are achieved:

- Continuity of existence.
- Limited liability.
- Centralized management.
- Flexibility.

The ultimate objective is this: with proper use of the Contractual Company, probate, death and inheritance taxes and capital gains tax may be avoided, and income tax may be substantially reduced.

The Contractual Company is, in short, a legal means of protecting what is rightfully yours, to be passed on to your heirs, rather than having the assets taken by the IRS or unscrupulous attorneys.

Characteristics of the Contractual Company

The Contractual Company is similar to a corporation in that both legal and equitable title or ownership go into the entity.

In most forms of trust, including grantor type trust, legal

ownership and equitable ownership are split. The legal ownership is vested in the entity or its trustee, and the equity is in the certificates of beneficial interest for the beneficiaries.

A business trust organization, or Massachusetts Business Trust Organization, is a type of trust called "pure trust" (as discussed in the previous chapter). The distinguishing feature is that both legal and equitable ownership go into the entity. There is no splitting of the ownership.

The Mesabi Iron Range is a Massachusetts Business Trust Organization. Its certificates of beneficial interest are traded on the New York Stock Exchange. The certificates of Mesabi are much the same as a stock certificate.

The Contractual Company has the following characteristics:

- No beneficiaries.
- No grantors.
- No certificates of beneficial interest.
- Managed by a trustee who appoints officers.
- Has only nonvoting capital units.
- Is formed under common law, not by statutory rules or laws made by legislation.
- Is not dependent upon a state or government for the granting of its existence.
- Can engage in any lawful business enterprise anywhere in the world.
- Not restricted as to how or what investments it can make.

The Contractual Company can be described as a common law entity, much like a common law corporation, which evolved from trust laws and practices.

Protecting Assets Through Common Law Right of Contract

From the dawn of civilization, history has recorded repetitive incidents of one man or several oppressing and plundering the rights and property of others.

It seems if man is to raise himself above the animal instinct of survival of the fittest, he must come to respect other men's property and rights.

The United States is a country founded upon the principle that life, liberty and property are sacred and are fully protected because these rights came not only from man's right in a state of nature to "exist," but also by the fact that man inherently received these rights from the Creator as inalienable rights—a nation under God, of the people, by the people and for the people.

Embodied in these principles is common law. Since common law recognizes inalienable rights and sets forth modes of proceedings in which common law rights can be enforced, it should consequently be in our interest to look to and use the common law of the land for the protection of our liberty and property. As a cornerstone of the foundation of all liberties, there lies the most precious and most priceless common law right of all. Were we without it, all other common law rights would be of little importance or of little consequence. That is the *common law right of contract.*

Both the accounting and legal institutions served man well for centuries but, it appears, their recent evolution has taken them into the realm of gluttonous racketeering. It sometimes appears that laws are made by lawyers for the legal and accounting professions. While the accounting profession provides a valuable statistical and recording function from which management can better function, the Internal Revenue Service rules have negated the benefits of that service by placing the emphasis on accounting for taxes rather than statistical purposes. Regarding the legal profession, one needs only to visit any municipal court on any Monday morning to get a glimpse of the dozens of poor people brought into court, fined and released in a much worse position than they were before, with less money and a greater fear and hatred for society. This activity can benefit no one other than the police industry and the gluttonous legal profession.

Who to trust or to rely upon regarding estate preservation is a decision only each individual can make. Ask your attorney or accountant—if you rely upon his advice, however you will most likely stay within the system which he knows and from which he profits. It is not intended that all attorneys or accountants be labeled as dishonest or self-serving. Many are not, but it is the opinion of many persons that they do not comprehend the effects of their actions upon individuals.

Many attorneys and accountants recommend the Contractual Company for privacy and tax avoidance, but generally after a thorough study of the method and at great expense. Once an attorney does become cognizant, he generally recommends it enthusiastically.

In tax matters, it should be noted, the legal profession has permitted many barriers to our constitutional right to trial by jury. This is true even though the Constitution is clear that in any civil matter involving $20 or more, the defendant has a right to trial by jury.

However, in tax matters, the individual must pay the entire amount of tax assessed by the Internal Revenue Service before embarking on a jury-heard suit in Federal Court to recover the money. Otherwise, the taxpayer's recourse is in a tax court where only a judge is allowed by law to hear the case. Many people believe that a tax court judge compromisingly weighs his opinions in favor of the Internal Revenue Service.

The Contractual Company Concept is Unique

Since the writing of the original document which creates the Contractual Company, I have had to make only minor changes. A title officer with a large title insurance company in California probably described the Contractual Company best when he said, "It is alien as far as standard types of business organizations are concerned. It's not a corporation, it's not exactly a trust, it's not a partnership. It is like nothing else. Yet it forms a separate, distinct legal entity."

That has been my belief from the beginning: that an entity could be created which could do the things necessary not only to preserve an estate but to enable the assets to be invested in the manner the trustees and officers choose, in stocks, bonds, real property, oil wells, limited partnerships, commodities and any other investments, and to comply with the U.S. tax code.

Hopefully, a new type of business entity in the form of Nassau Life Insurance Company's *Contractual Company* has been discovered. A federal judge has upheld the Contractual Company document as forming a legal company, in his ruling in U.S. v. Brownlee, as further discussed in the legal opinions in Chapter XIV.

The following is a step-by-step explanation of exactly how an offshore Contractual Company can be formed, how it can be used and how it will result in substantial—and legal!—tax savings for an individual American taxpayer.

Formation of the Companies

All companies are formed in the same manner, just as all corporations are formed in the same manner but by a set of regulations passed by a state legislature. Most states have a standard prescribed set of forms by which a corporation is formed.

The Contractual Company is formed as follows:

1. First, a name is selected for the company.
2. The contract which forms the company is written.
3. The contract is then signed before a notary public in the Turks and Caicos Islands by the following:
   a. The Creator
   b. The Exchanger

Role of the Creator

The creator, who is a Turks and Caicos Islands citizen, could be compared to the witness at a wedding or the incorporators of a corporation. Once the necessary documents are signed at the wedding, the witness no longer has a function to serve. It is the same with the incorporators of a corporation. The signatures of the incorporators are absolutely required to form the entity, but once the entity is formed there is no further function to be served. This is the same as with the creator, who has no function in the company once he has signed his name and the company is formed.

Role of the Exchanger

The next person involved is the *exchanger.* The exchanger must also be a foreign person. When this company was organized, it had absolutely no assets. It is like all companies when they are first formed; they have nothing, except, if the company is a corporation, it would have shares for sale. In this case, the company has one hundred capital units. This is the only way the company has of acquiring assets, of obtaining money with which to operate. This is where the exchanger enters the picture: the exchanger is the person who puts in the first assets (remember, when we formed the company, it had *no* assets). The exchanger puts in $100 and receives back one hundred capital units. But the exchanger keeps only *one* of those capital

The Contractual Company is formed in the following manner in the Turks and Caicos Islands, B.W.I. (a British crown colony).

The name of the Company is selected. We will use the name Atlantic Investment Company in the example.

Exchange (for 99 units) stocks, bonds, cash, other assets (if any) plus a promissory note in the amount of $100,000 at 10% interest. If the interest is paid a $10,000 passive investment interest expense deduction is achieved.

Atlantic Investment Company

100 Capital Units

The Company is a separate judicial or legal entity. It can do anything that you a live breathing person can do in the way of owning, buying, selling, etc.

The Company is formed by Turks and Caicos Island residents as follows:

Creator — like the incorporator of a corporation or the witness at a wedding—significant only for the beginning.

Exchangor—1st unit holder puts $100.00 into Company—receives 100 units—sells back 99 units to Company—keeps one unit for legal reasons—you exchange note, cash and other assets for 99 units.

Trustee—Nassau Life Insurance Company, Limited. Like board of directors in corporation. Trustee appoints you Agent President. You will also need an Agent Secretary. You may want Vice Presidents and a Treasurer but they are not necessary to operate the Company. Only a President and Secretary are required.

units. He approaches the trustee of the company and he *sells back* to the company the ninety-nine remaining units. Those are the ninety-nine units that the client, the person for whom we are forming the Contractual Company, would end up holding.

It is important that the exchanger keep that one capital unit in the company. The reason is this: the situation could conceivably arise wherein there would need to be a lawsuit filed in the U.S.; because of what the Constitution says about federal courts, chances are the foreign trustee and the foreign exchanger could file that suit and the U.S. taxpayer would stay totally uninvolved.

Although the exchanger keeps only that one unit of the company assets, he knows that someone might be a little bit concerned with him owning even one percent of the company's assets (one unit out of one hundred capital units being one percent of the company's assets). For instance, if this Contractual Company had $10 million in assets, the exchanger would technically own one percent of it, or $100,000. This point of concern is handled this way: the exchanger says, "I will give you an indefinite, irrevocable option to repurchase that one unit for $10." At any time in the future you can buy that one unit back from the exchanger for $10. Meanwhile, however, it is his and he owns it while he holds it—with the expressed understanding that you have the indefinite, irrevocable option to buy it back for $10 *at any time*.

The Foreign Trustee

The next person involved in the company would be the *trustee*. The trustee also must be a foreign person. Let me cite a personal experience in explaining why this is important. One of my chief attorneys in San Francisco recently attended the retirement party of a senior attorney for the IRS. The IRS attorney was asked about the IRS position on offshore trust organizations, and his comment was, "As long as there's a foreign trustee, there's darn little we can do about them." Obviously, that's the kind of position we like to have the IRS in—so we must have the foreign trustee for this company. In this case, the foreign trustee would be Nassau Life Insurance Company, Ltd.

Now that the documents have been signed before the notary public, the company has been formed.

The trustee declares the contract to be in full force and commences to operate under the contract. The trustee appoints officers to act for the company.

While the company has the legal right to do everything that a live, breathing person can do, it is helpless to act on its own. It cannot think. The trustee must think for it. The company cannot walk, talk or write its name, so someone must do those things for it. The officers do those functions, assigned by the trustee to the respective officers, for the company.

The President

Nassau Life Insurance Company, Ltd., as the foreign trustee, acting much like a board of directors in a corporation, appoints someone to the office of president. In the formal documents for the company, the president, as is the case with all officers of the company, is appointed the "Nonexclusive Agent President." This distinction is important. The U.S. tax code has specific rules relating to nonexclusive agents and for that reason you are appointed Nonexclusive Agent President of the company. The title of Nonexclusive Agent President doesn't mean that this company can have a lot of presidents. It simply means that you can be president of other companies; you're not exclusively the president or agent for this company.

There is an important reason for being a Nonexclusive

Agent officer: we do not want this company effectively connected with U.S. trade or commerce. If it should become effectively connected with U.S. trade or commerce, the company might have to fill out tax returns. But, as long as the officers are serving as a Nonexclusive Agents in the U.S., the company does not become effectively connected with U.S. trade or commerce, as it might if the company had exclusive agents. Under the U.S. tax code, a foreign company can have information offices or warehouses in the U.S. without being effectively connected with U.S. trade or commerce.

The Secretary

There is one other person necessary for this company to operate and that is a *secretary*.

The signatures of the president and the secretary are all that are required for buying, selling, opening bank accounts or stock brokerage accounts, and signing contracts.

Other officers may be appointed as vice presidents or treasurer. Assistants to those officers may also be appointed.

Since the people exchanging the property or assets into the Contractual Company are the ones most familiar with the assets, they are logically the ones best qualified to assist the trustee in managing those assets.

Frequently the husband and wife who exchange assets into the company are appointed the president and secretary. Sometimes other family members are appointed to offices of the company to replace the president and secretary upon death or incapacitation.

The First Contingent Trustee

First Contingent Trustee of the company is appointed. If the foreign trustee, Nassau Life Insurance Company, Ltd., falls into the ocean or goes bankrupt, the first obligation that Nassau Life would have, as foreign trustee, would be to see that another trustee is appointed. This could be another organization that would be willing to act as foreign trustee if for some reason Nassau Life was no longer able to do so. The officers could become the trustee if Nassau Life ceased to exist—but only long enough to select another *foreign* trustee for the company. This might take no longer than 30 to 90 days and could be accomplished without doing any harm at all to the system or endangering the status of the Contractual Company under the provisions of the U.S. tax code regarding offshore companies with foreign trustees.

Second Contingent Trustees are Frequently Appointed

We also need a *second* set of *Contingent Trustees*. If the First Contingent Trustees, the husband and wife, for example, were to depart for heaven at the same time, then we would need Second Contingent Trustees who could take over the company. These should be the people who would manage the assets of the company. For example, the children of the First Contingent Trustees might logically be named as Second Contingent Trustees. Then, upon the death of the First Contingent Trustees, the Second Contingent Trustees—in this case the children of the husband and wife who were the Nonexclusive Agent President and the Secretary—would automatically assume the positions held by the first contingents.

By naming the second set of Contingent Trustees and by having directed the company's trustee to whom to issue the new certificates upon the death of the original owner, the necessity for a will would be eliminated.

Replacing the Foreign Trustee

Nassau Life Insurance Company, Ltd., as foreign trustee of the Contractual Company, could be replaced if it failed to control or manage the assets properly. For that reason, Nassau Life includes in the company documents a *signed, undated resignation* as foreign trustee of the company. If a date was placed on that document Nassau Life would immediately be removed as foreign trustee.

This is a common practice in many corporations. If a president appoints a person to a high position, such as vice president, he will ask for an undated letter of resignation at the time that person is appointed. It is also done in government. When a person is appointed to a high position in the government, out of courtesy he tenders his resignation to the president or prime minister, so that if the president or prime minister is not satisfied with the person's performance at some point in the future, all he has to do is put a date on the pre-arranged letter of resignation and announce that Mr. So-and-so has tendered his resignation, effective on a certain date, or perhaps immediately, and that it has been accepted. When in fact what the president or prime minister had done was put into effect an undated letter of resignation given at the time of the person's appointment to the position. Stern vs. Commissioner validates our position on the undated resignation.

Forming Other Companies

Now, after the first company is formed, a whole series of other companies can be formed.

Each of these other companies would have to have a name. So we will give them the following names:

- The Home Company
- The Lease Company

- The Management Company
- The Trading Company
- The Apartment Company
- The Investment Company

Each one of these companies, just like the first company, has one hundred capital units. And just as we did when forming the first company, the exchanger keeps one unit and the ninety-nine remaining units are held by the second exchanger.

Using the Home Company

First, let's examine the uses of the Home Company. Let's assume you own a house and that house cost $50,000 when you bought it ten years ago. Today, it is worth $200,000. If you sold your house, you would have to pay a capital gains tax based on the $200,000 sale price. If you made a gift of the house to the Home Company, you would still have to pay a gift tax on the $50,000. We don't want either of those contingencies to occur. So what is done is this: the house is *exchanged* into the Home Company. In this exchange we must receive something back, or otherwise it would be considered a gift. So what we receive back is the key to this transaction: a certificate for the ninety-nine capital units of the Home Company. This certificate, according to the U.S. tax code, must have value. It cannot be worthless. On the other hand, the value of this certificate *must be* indeterminable. So the value of this certificate for the ninety-nine capital units from the Home Company *does have value*, but the value is indeterminable.

IRS agents have in the past taken a long, hard look at certificates of this type and said, "Wait a minute! We know the value of the home is $200,000, so we're going to say the value of the certificate is $200,000." But the U.S. Supreme Court has ruled time after time that the value of

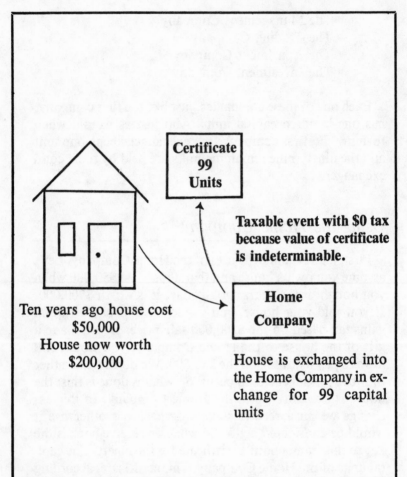

Certificate 99 Units

Taxable event with $0 tax because value of certificate is indeterminable.

Ten years ago house cost
$50,000
House now worth
$200,000

Home Company

House is exchanged into the Home Company in exchange for 99 capital units

If house is gifted to the Home Company, gift tax must be paid.

If house is sold to the Home company, capital gains tax will be incurred.

House transferred by either quit claim, warranty or grant deed. I prefer to use same deed form to transfer property to Contractual Company as the Exchangor currently has, i.e. the same form by which he received property.

the home has nothing to do with it. A person is taxed based upon what he *receives*. What he received was a certificate, not dollars. He received a certificate with an indeterminable value. The Supreme Court has further said that while this might actually be an economic gain, it cannot possibly be considered a taxable gain until the person actually receives the money. If he sells the certificate at a later time, or if he receives a distribution, he would then have to pay taxes in the U.S. on the gain from the sale of the certificate or the income from the distribution.

When we put the house into the Home Company, we would at the same time put the furniture, antiques, jewelry and other personal items of value into the Home Company.

Using the Lease Company

We would exchange into the Lease Company high-risk items, such as automobiles, boats and motorcycles. These are items with a high-liability risk attached to them. We don't want assets such as a home to be at stake, as it is for the unprotected individual involved in an accident. In the event of an accident the only assets that could be gotten from the Lease Company would be those held by the Lease Company. Each of the companies is a separate legal or judicial entity. What we are achieving by forming more than one entity is not only limited liability, but we are achieving compartmentalized liability. Assets held by the Home Company would not be at risk if an automobile owned by the Lease Company was involved in an accident. Only the assets held by the Lease company could be taken by a lawsuit.

There are other uses for the Lease Company. Let's assume that there is a machine shop with a lot of expensive machinery. The machines can be exchanged into the Lease Company in exchange for a certificate of indeterminable value. The

What Goes Into Which Company

Home Company	Lease Company

Home   Automobiles
Furnishings   Motorcycles
Paintings   Machinery
Antiques   Airplanes
Jewelry   High-risk items
Clothing   Items to be leased back for
                        use by U.S. taxpayer

Apartment Or Management Company	Investment Company

Rental property   Stocks
Businesses   Bonds
Leasehold Investments   Gold
                        Silver
                        Diamonds
                        Cash
                        Investments of any kind
                        Personal note in the amount of
                        $100,000 at 10% interest

All assets are exchanged into the Companies in exchange for 99 capital units.

The assets also may be exchanged into the Companies in exchange for a combination of 99 units plus notes receivable.

machinery can then be leased back. The lease payments to the nonresident alien company could be deducted from the tax returns of the lessee.

Using the Apartment Company

The Apartment Company is where we put rental properties, buildings and land. Let's assume that one hundred rental units are exchanged for the ninety-nine capital units of the Apartment Company. If the Apartment Company actually rents those to one hundred different individuals, there is no question but what the company would be effectively connected with U.S. trade or commerce. What could be done in this case is to form either a domestic company, or take a live, breathing person, to whom the company would lease all one hundred rental units. That one U.S. company, or live, breathing person, would then lease back the one hundred units, then rent them to individuals. The U.S. entity would be required to comply with all the U.S. tax rules and regulations such as payroll withholding. Any profit left at the end of the year earned by the U.S. entity would necessitate filing a tax return and paying taxes on that profit. But the offshore company, because there is only the one lease, would not be effectively connected with U.S. trade or commerce, and therefore the offshore company would not be required to file a tax return.

Using the Investment Company

The Investment Company is where we put our stocks, bonds, gold, silver, trust deeds, cash and other investments. The documents which form the companies have been approved by all major brokerage firms for opening accounts. The one we like the best and use the most is Shearson, which

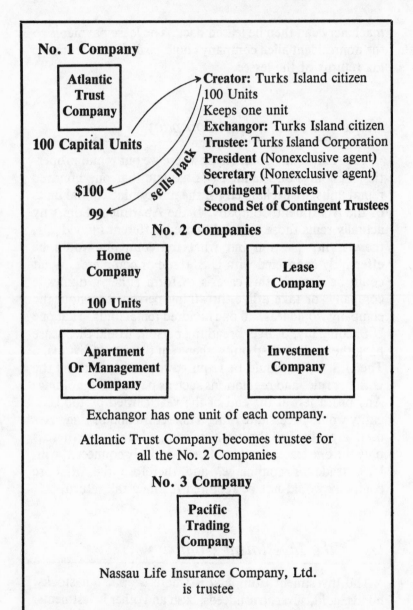

No. 1 Company

Atlantic
Trust
Company

100 Capital Units

$100

99

sells back

Creator: Turks Island citizen
100 Units
Keeps one unit
Exchangor: Turks Island citizen
Trustee: Turks Island Corporation
President (Nonexclusive agent)
Secretary (Nonexclusive agent)
Contingent Trustees
Second Set of Contingent Trustees

No. 2 Companies

Home
Company

100 Units

Lease
Company

Apartment
Or Management
Company

Investment
Company

Exchangor has one unit of each company.

Atlantic Trust Company becomes trustee for
all the No. 2 Companies

No. 3 Company

Pacific
Trading
Company

Nassau Life Insurance Company, Ltd.
is trustee

This arrangement is used for arranging complex estates.
It eliminates the necessity for a Will.

is now the largest brokerage firm in the U.S. We have had the legal departments of Shearson and other major brokerage firms examine our documents and approve them for opening accounts. Thousands of our clients have accounts with major U.S. brokerage firms wherein the Agent President of the offshore company can call that firm and instruct them to buy a hundred shares of AT&T or a thousand shares of DuPont, whatever it might be, on behalf of the Investment Company. There is no capital gains tax to pay on the earnings because this is a nonresident alien company. Since the Deficit Reduction Act of 1984, interest and dividends are also excluded from taxation in the U.S. Investments are virtually tax-free when made by this nonresident company.

A $10,000 passive investment interest expense deduction may be achieved through the Investment Company simply by exchanging a personal promissory note into the Investment Company in exchange for the ninety-nine capital units. The personal note payable to the company may be exchanged into the company along with a portfolio of stocks, bonds and other investments, or the note could be the only item exchanged. The note could be in the amount of $100,000 at 10 percent interest. If the interest is actually paid by a U.S. taxpayer, he may deduct the $10,000 passive interest expense from his taxable income. The following excerpt from the IRS tax code documents the legal status of such investment interest deductions:

I.R.S. TAX CODE

A. INVESTMENT INTEREST DEDUCTION
$10,000 ($5,000 in the case of a separate return by a married individual). Code section 163. Interest deduction (d)(1)(A)
B. INTEREST TAX FREE TO NON-RESIDENT ALIEN

Department of the Treasury—Internal Revenue Service
Publication 901 (Rev. No. 81)

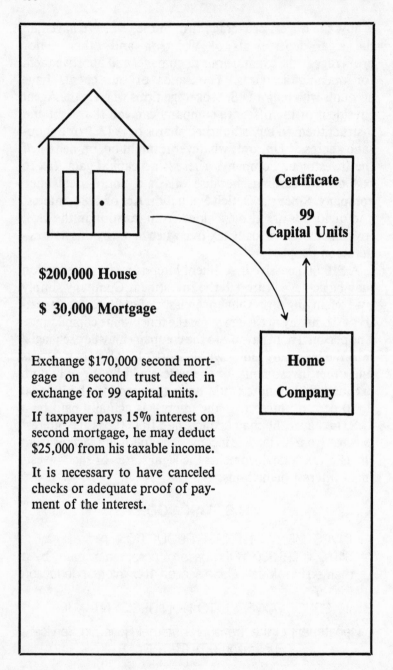

$200,000 House

$ 30,000 Mortgage

Exchange $170,000 second mortgage on second trust deed in exchange for 99 capital units.

If taxpayer pays 15% interest on second mortgage, he may deduct $25,000 from his taxable income.

It is necessary to have canceled checks or adequate proof of payment of the interest.

U.S. Tax Treaties

Introduction

The United States has income tax treaties (conventions) with a number of foreign countries. Under these treaties residents (sometimes limited to citizens) of foreign countries are taxed at a reduced rate or are exempt from U.S. income taxes on certain amounts of income they receive from within the United States. These reduced rates and exemptions vary between countries and specific items of income.

Interest

If you are a nonresident alien who receives interest that is not effectively connected with the conduct of a U.S. trade or business, you do not have to include the interest in income if it is paid on deposits by banks, on deposits or accounts by certain financial institutions, and on certain amounts held by insurance companies. Under the Internal Revenue Code, these amounts are treated as foreign source income and are exempt from U.S. tax. See Publication 519, U.S. Tax Guide for Aliens.

Gift Taxes

Your question at this point might well be, "How do I get money back out of these companies? How does some of this come back to wherever I want it to go in the U.S.?"

One method that could be used is receiving from the companies certain gifts of an intangible nature. This, for instance, is what the U.S. tax code has to say about gifts of an intangible nature from a foreign source:

C. NO GIFT TAXES—NO ESTATE TAXES

Department of the Treasury—Internal Revenue Service
Publication 448 (Rev. May 1982)

Federal Estate and Gift Taxes

Location of Property

Property located in the United States. For a decedent who at death was a nonresident noncitizen, property is considered located in the United

States if it is:

1) Real property located in the United States.
2) Tangible personal property located in the United States. This includes clothing, jewelry, automobiles, furniture, or currency. Works of art imported into the United States solely for public exhibition purposes are not included.
3) A debt obligation of a citizen or resident of the United States, a domestic partnership or corporation, any estate or trust (but not a foreign estate or trust), the United States, a state, or a political subdivision of a state, or the District of Columbia (however, see the exceptions in the following paragraphs), or
4) Shares of stock issued by domestic corporation.

Nonresident noncitizen. For an individual who is neither a citizen nor a resident of the United States, the federal gift tax applies only to gifts of property situated within the United States. If an individual is a resident of a U.S. possession at the time of the gift and is a U.S. citizen only because of birth, residence, or citizenship in that possession, he or she is considered a nonresident noncitizen for gift tax purposes. A gift of intangible personal property is not subject to federal gift tax if it is made by a nonresident non-citizen, except in the case of certain expatriate U.S. citizens. (See Gifts by Nonresident Noncitizen.)

Property not located in the United States. Notwithstanding the above rules, property of a nonresident noncitizen decedent is not considered located in the United States if it is:

1) A deposit with a U.S. bank, if the deposit was not connected with a U.S. trade or business and was paid or credited to the decedent's account.
2) A deposit or withdrawable account with a savings and loan association chartered and supervised under federal or state law or an amount held by an insurance company under an agreement to pay interest on it. But the deposit or amount must not be connected with a U.S. trade or business and must be paid or credited to the decedent's account.
3) A deposit with a foreign branch of a U.S. bank, if the branch is engaged in the commercial banking business.

Congress, in this instance, was wise enough to recognize that its jurisdiction ends at the U.S. borders, that it cannot pass laws regarding, for instance, Turks and Caicos Islands people. And here is an important point: all of these companies that we have formed are like people; they can do

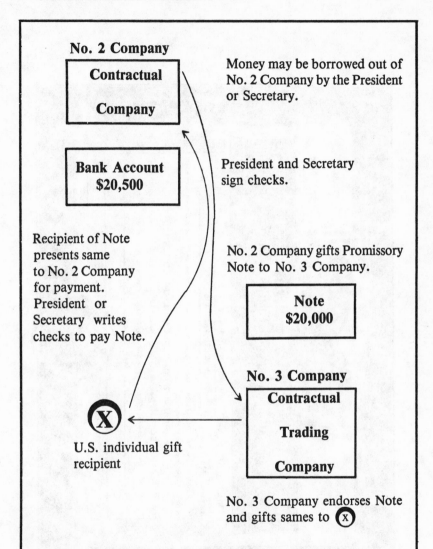

No. 2 Company

Contractual

Company

Money may be borrowed out of No. 2 Company by the President or Secretary.

Bank Account $20,500

President and Secretary sign checks.

Recipient of Note presents same to No. 2 Company for payment. President or Secretary writes checks to pay Note.

No. 2 Company gifts Promissory Note to No. 3 Company.

Note $20,000

No. 3 Company

Contractual

Trading

Company

U.S. individual gift recipient

No. 3 Company endorses Note and gifts sames to (x)

The Note is an intangible. The gift is from a totally foreign source.

Gift must be of an intangible nature from a foreign source in order to avoid tax.

Money may not be intangible since it is a medium of exchange or a call upon goods or services which are tangible or real.

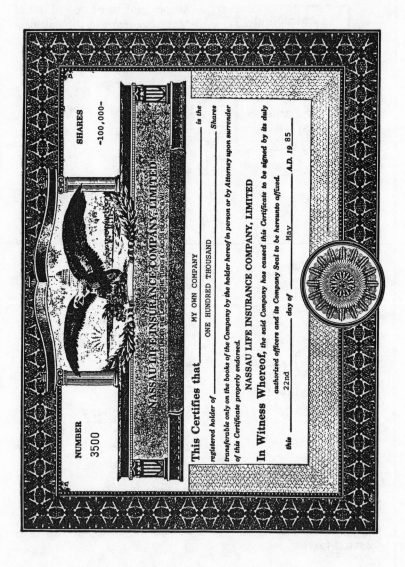

anything that a person can do, except they can't walk or talk and, most important of all, they can't think. The officers and the trustees have to do the thinking and acting for them. But the U.S. government realizes that this nonresident alien company cannot be made to pay a gift tax. *There is no legal way that the IRS can tax gifts of an intangible nature from foreign sources.* "Intangible" is the key word here and one that needs to be defined. There is a tax court case that says money is not intangible, that money is indeed a tangible item. The court held that money is a call on goods or services that are tangible or real; therefore, money is tangible since it is a medium of exchange. So we cannot give money—but we can give notes, stocks, bonds, those items that have been determined by the courts to be intangible. And of course everyone knows that you don't pay taxes on borrowed money, so you could borrow money from any one of these companies and not pay taxes on the money you borrow.

The Cost of Forming
A Contractual Company Arrangement

Normally, the cost of forming a complete Contractual Company arrangement involving six companies to adequately protect the assets would be in the neighborhood of $14,000. The annual trustee fee of $750 is included in that price for the first year. However, everyone doesn't need a complete Contractual Company arrangement. Some estates might require only three companies. Others might need only one company. If the estate consists of only stocks, bonds and investments, only one company may be required. A knowledgeable trust officer can determine exactly how many companies an estate needs during the interviews and discussions before actually forming the Contractual Company arrangement. For each company formed, when taken as individual companies, the cost is $2,800 per company. That includes the first year's trustee fee of $250.

The Contractual Company

CONTRACT

THIS DOCUMENT, EXECUTED UNDER THE LAWS OF THE

TURKS AND CAICOS ISLANDS, BRITISH WEST INDIES,

A BRITISH CROWN COLONY,

BY COMMON LAW RIGHT OF CONTRACT CREATES

<u>XYZ INVESTMENT COMPANY</u>

WITH NASSAU LIFE INSURANCE COMPANY, LTD.

AS TRUSTEE,

THIS FIFTEENTH DAY OF MAY, 1985

Documentary stamps

NASSAU LIFE INSURANCE COMPANY, LTD.
ADMINISTRATION OFFICE

Dear Agent Officers:

Enclosed please find the documents for the Company which you have
been selected to represent as Agent President and Agent Secretary.   It is not necessary that you delve too deeply into the
complex legal and accounting matters; however, you may wish to
learn more about the Companies as a matter of interest.

The basic facts are as follows:

Assets may be exchanged into the Company for Certificates of
indeterminable value.

After the exchange is made the assets exchanged should be listed
on Schedules A and B at the back of the document.   Real Estate
should be listed on Schedule A.   Everything else, stocks, bonds,
cash, autos, etc. should be listed on Schedule B.   It is not
necessary to place a value on the assets.

The Company is formed by a Creator who is a Foreign Person, an
Exchangor who is also a Foreign Person, and a Trustee-Nassau Life
Insurance Company, Ltd.

The Company does not file a tax return unless it is engaged in
U.S. trade or commerce. Buying commodities, stocks, bonds, etc.
does not engage the Company in U.S. trade or commerce.   This is
passive income. You are the nonexclusive Agents for the Company.

This means that you may represent 100 or more Companies.   If you
were the exclusive agents, this factor might be construed to mean
that the Company, because of exclusive agents, would be effectively connected, or engaged in U.S. trade or commerce.

Gifts of an intangible nature are excluded in the gift tax
section of the Internal Revenue Code.   Also you do not pay taxes
on money loaned or advanced to you by the Company.

If you file U.S. tax return, Schedule B has two questions which must be considered:

1. Are you a signator of a foreign bank account?
    ANSWER: "NO"

2. Have you contributed property to a foreign trust?
    ANSWER: "NO"

    According to I.R.S. definition, this is not a foreign trust.

ATTENTION: TO OPEN A BANK ACCOUNT - SEE ATTACHED

Record keeping may be as simple as you like. Cancelled checks and stubs along with confirmations and receipts are all that are needed except for your own statistical purposes.

Schedules A and B should show the assets exchanged for the Certificates. It is a good idea to include a large personal note from yourself to the Company so you will have a means of putting funds in after the initial exchange. You may deduct the interest on the note from personal taxes if you actually pay interest to the Company.

PLEASE NOTE: You should never show the Company Contracts to the I.R.S. without first contacting Nassau Life Insurance Company, Ltd. at P.M.B. 11, Grand Turk, Turks and Caicos Islands, B.W.I. Nassau Life Insurance Company, Ltd. is the Trustee and the one who would deal with the I.R.S. regarding Trust Documents, Taxes, etc. You are required only to present your side of each transaction, meaning what you put in or what you received back. (Receipts, Certificates, etc.).

You may call us at any time for assistance. In case you can not find a U.S. representative, the permanent address is the same for Nassau Life Insurance Company, Ltd. as for your Companies: P.M.B. 11, Grand Turk, Turks and Caicos Islands, B.W.I.

You should use the foreign address when opening brokerage accounts. If your broker gives you any difficulty, you can use Shearson/American Express.

Please call me if you have any question.

Sincerely,

ROBERT CHAPPELL

PROCEDURE FOR OPENING A BANK ACCOUNT:

If you are not known at the bank, or if you are not with someone who can verify your identity, you may be asked for some form of identification: DRIVER'S LICENSE, CREDIT CARD, etc.

It is advisable that you remove the Financial Institution Minute (located near the back of your Number 2 and Number 3 Companies) and the Certificate of Incorporation for Nassau Life Insurance Company, Ltd. (located near the front of your Number 1 Company) from your contract. It is neither necessary nor advisable to take your full set of documents with you when you open your account.

PRIOR TO THE TIME YOU WISH TO OPEN YOUR ACCOUNT:

(a) Go to the Bank and pick up a Bank-Depositor Agreement. (Ask for Corporate Bank Form) Fill out the Agreement.

YOUR TAX IDENTIFICATION NUMBER IS 98-0051978

(b) Have a Cashier's Check made payable to your Company in the amount equal to, or greater than, the Bank's minimum requirement for the opening of said account. Having a Cashier's Check in lieu of Cash adds more professionalism and credibility to the transaction.

When you go into open your Account, just state that you wish to open a Company Account. This is a private investment type of an account as you will not be engaged in business or commerce nor will you be contacting the public for any monies.

TAKE THESE ITEMS WITH YOU TO THE BANK:

(a) Completed Bank-Depositor Agreement
(b) Cashier's Check
(c) Financial Institution Minute (BE SURE THAT THE MINUTE IS SIGNED BY THE OFFICERS OF YOUR COMPANY.) The Bank will probably want this for its file. Just request that a copy be made for the bank file; you keep the original.
(d) Nassau Life Insurance Company, Ltd. Certificate of Incorporation and Trustee Resolution.
(e) Company Seal

TO WHOM IT MAY CONCERN

THE COMPANIES ORDINANCE 1981

CERTIFICATE OF GOOD STANDING

This is to Certify that

NASSAU LIFE INSURANCE COMPANY LIMITED

incorporated under the Companies Ordinance 1981 on the

25th day of JANUARY 1978 is in good standing

with this Office at the date hereof.

Given under my hand and seal this 14th day of MAY 1984

RAYMOND HARVEY CHECKLEY
Registrar of Companies

Registered No. 836

TURKS & CAICOS ISLANDS

THE COMPANIES ORDINANCE 1971

CERTIFICATE OF INCORPORATION

"NASSAU LIFE INSURANCE COMPANY LIMITED"

....

is this day incorporated under the Companies Ordinance 1971 as a Limited

Liability Company.

Dated 25th   day of January, 19 78

Registrar of Companies.
ENA J. C. WOODSTOCK.

Registered No. 836.

CERTIFICATE

I, ENA J. C. WOODSTOCK Registrar of Companies for the Turks and Caicos Islands, do hereby certify that the requirements of the Companies Ordinance 1971 in respect of:

"NASSAU LIFE INSURANCE COMPANY LIMITED"

have been complied with.

I, do further certify that the Memorandum and Articles of Association in respect of this Company were recorded on the 25th day of January, 1978 on page 213 of Book "B" of the Public Records of the Register of Companies.

REGISTRAR OF COMPANIES
ENA J. C. WOODSTOCK.

BOARD OF DIRECTORS' MEETING

February 1, 1978

NASSAU LIFE INSURANCE COMPANY, LIMITED

Pursuant to call, a Special Meeting of the Board of Directors of Nassau Life Insurance Company, Limited was called to order at the Company's Home Office, Miramar Building, Queen Street, Grand Turks, Turks and Caicos islands, on the 1st day of February, 1978.

The Secretary read the Minutes of the previous meeting. Upon motion, the Minutes were approved unanimously as read.

The Chairman of the Board proposed the following:

Resolved, that Nassau Life Insurance Company, Ltd. become the Trustee for various business Trust Organizations and/or Trusts to be organized, and to perform any and all functions of that position, for fees to be negotiated and determined by the Chairman and Company President, for any Trust or business Trust Organization to which the Company shall be appointed Trustee.

Further resolved, that Robert Chappell be and hereby is empowered to carry out said function and to sign any and all documents on behalf of the Company pertaining thereto and to appoint assistants for the same said purpose.

The motion was seconded by Marilyn V. Turner Carmichael, the Company Secretary and Director. Upon vote, the motion carried unanimously.

There being no further business to come before the board, the Chairman adjourned the meeting.

Robert Chappell
Chairman

Marilyn V. Turner Carmichael
Secretary

A BUSINESS TRUST ORGANIZATION

1.   This contract is made MAY 15, 1985 by and between WALTER R. SIMONS of Grand Turk, Turks and Caicos Islands, British West Indies, hereinafter termed the CREATOR, and CYNTHIA A. FRANCIS (of above address), hereinafter termed the EXCHANGOR.

2.   By this document, a common law contractual business trust organization is established pursuant to all of the conditions contained herein with certain assets to be administered by a Trustee for Certificate Holders under the name of:

XYZ INVESTMENT COMPANY

hereinafter termed the COMPANY.

3.   The Company shall be domiciled at Grand Turk, Turks and Caicos Islands, B.W.I. However, a change of situs may be ordered by the Trustee in the event of war, riot, insurrection, or political change.

4.   This Company shall not operate as a partnership, association, joint venture, joint stock company, corporation, or statutory trust. It shall be construed to be a common law contractual business trust organization.

5.   The Company, through its Trustee, shall allocate 100 Capital Units contained in the organization in the form of Certificates to be issued to Exchangor for property exchanged.

6.   The CREATOR approached the EXCHANGOR and offered to

1

exchange One Dollar ($1.00) and a Certificate for 100 Capital Units of this business trust organization for personal property, to wit: the sum of One Hundred Dollars ($100.00). It was agreed by the parties hereto that this was neither a gift nor a sale. The offer was accepted and the exchange consummated.

7.   The CREATOR hereby appoints NASSAU LIFE INSURANCE COMPANY, LTD. of Grand Turk, Turks and Caicos Islands, B.W.I., as the TRUSTEE. NASSAU LIFE INSURANCE COMPANY, LTD., for and in consideration of the sum of One Dollar ($1.00) and for fees and remuneration now agreed and to be set forth in Minutes of the Trust Organization, hereby accepts the appointment on the terms herein.

8.   The Trustee, NASSAU LIFE INSURANCE COMPANY, LTD., shall control and administer all assets of the Company to the best of its ability for the Certificate Holders.

9.   The Trustee shall stand by appointment in trust irrevocable at the service to the Company.

10.   The Company shall endure for twenty-five years from the date of this document and may be renewed for like periods prior to the expiration of each twenty-five year period by action of the Trustees. Unless so renewed, the corpus of the Company shall be distributed to the Certificate Holders.

11.   The Trustee may resign on 30-day's notice without cause. Upon resigning, the Trustee shall immediately appoint the first named successor Trustee from a list of successor Trustee(s) previously designated in a Trust Minute. The successor Trustee

shall assume the duties and reponsibilities of Trustee on the expiration date of the outgoing Trustee. Upon the death or incapacity of the Trustee, the first listed successor Trustee named in the Trust Minute shall immediately assume the duties and responsibilities of Trustee, or he may appoint an alternate Trustee to serve in his stead. However, only on the death, incapacity, or resignation of a Trustee may a replacement Trustee be appointed.

12.   The Trustee may appoint agents who may be given the title of President, Vice-President, Secretary, or Treasurer to conduct the normal business affairs of the Company on behalf of the Trustee. The Trustee shall set reasonable compensation for such agents.

13.   The Trustee may employ outside accountants, attorney(s) and consultants, or management firms and pay reasonable compensation or fees for their service.

14.   The Trustee shall bear no personal liability for losses to the Company caused through Trustee's action made in good faith, nor for any claims or obligations however arising.

15.   The Company may engage in any type of business activity which the Trustee deems in the best interest of the Company, including, but not limited to, buying, selling, borrowing, loaning, pledging or hypothecating assets, and owning stock or entire charters of corporations, partnerships, associations, and trusts.

16.   Any question arising as to the validity, purport or intent of this document shall be interpreted in accordance with

the laws of the Turks and Caicos Islands, B.W.I.

17.   The Company shall provide for the issuance and transfer of Unit Capital Certificates. Such Certificates shall be in all respects personal property.   The Certificate Holders may there-fore elect to sell, gift, or exchange ownership of their Certifi-cates at any time as per their signed and dated instructions to be entered on the reverse of their certificates.

18.   The Trustee shall issue new Certificates in accordance with the instructions given by Certificate Holders or by their own decision in the absence of proper instructions issued before the death of a Certificate Holder.

19.   In every written contract, investment, or obligation given or executed by the Trustee on behalf of the Company or under his authority, it shall be the duty of the Trustee to insert or cause to be inserted therein a clause to the effect that the Certificate Holders shall not be personally liable for any debt, demand, or liability incurred by or under the authority of the Trustee and reference shall be made to this document. However, the failure of the Trustee or the agents of the Company to comply with the above provisions shall in no way be construed to render any Certificate Holder personally liable.

20.   A Certificate Holder shall have no right or title to, possession of, management of, or control over the assets of the Company.

21.   No person, heir, or devisee of any Certificate Holder shall have any right of dower, homestead or inheritance, or of

4

partition or of any other right, statutory or otherwise in any property whatever forming a part of this Company. The title, both legal and equitable, to all Company assets shall be vested in the Trustee. The sole interest of the Certificate Holders shall be their right to distributions made by action of the Trustee, or their share of the assets as shown by their Capital Units or Certificate payable upon dissolution of the Company.

22.   The death, insolvency, or bankruptcy of any Certificate Holder or Trustee shall not operate as a dissolution or affect the continuance of this organization.

23.   This document, together with the Trustee's minutes, constitutes the full agreement between the CREATOR, EXCHANGOR, and Certificate Holders and Trustee.

24.   The effective date and execution of this contract is MAY 15, 1985 at Grand Turk Island, Turks and Caicos Islands, B. W. I.

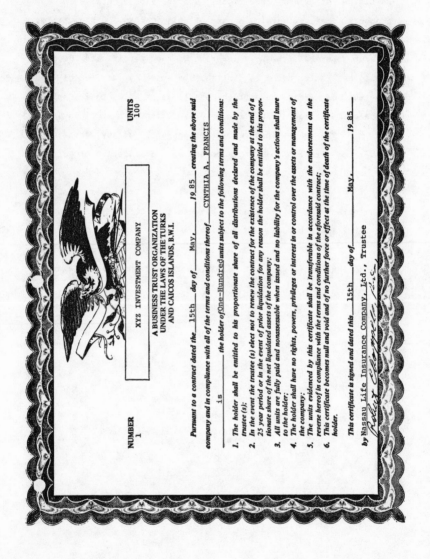

NUMBER
1

UNITS
100

XYZ INVESTMENT COMPANY

A BUSINESS TRUST ORGANIZATION
UNDER THE LAWS OF THE TURKS
AND CAICOS ISLANDS, B.W.I.

Pursuant to a contract dated the 15th day of May, 19 85 creating the above said company and in compliance with all of the terms and conditions thereof CYNTHIA A. FRANCIS

is the holder of One-Hundred units subject to the following terms and conditions:

1. The holder shall be entitled to his proportionate share of all distributions declared and made by the trustee (s);

2. In the event the trustee (s) elect not to renew the contract for the existence of the company at the end of a 25 year period or in the event of prior liquidation for any reason the holder shall be entitled to his proportionate share of the net liquidated assets of the company;

3. All units are fully paid and nonassessable when issued and no liability for the company's actions shall inure to the holder;

4. The holder shall have no rights, powers, privileges or interest in or control over the assets or management of the company;

5. The units evidenced by this certificate shall be transferable in accordance with the endorsement on the reverse hereof in compliance with the terms and conditions of the aforesaid contract;

6. This certificate becomes null and void and of no further force or effect at the time of death of the certificate holder.

This certificate is signed and dated this 15th day of May, 19 85

by Nassau Life Insurance Company, Ltd., Trustee

For value received,_____ hereby sell, assign and transfer unto

_____

PLEASE PRINT OR TYPEWRITE NAME AND ADDRESS OF ASSIGNEE

_____

_____

_____ Units
represented by the within Certificate, and do hereby irrevocably constitute
and appoint _____

Attorney to transfer the said units on the books of the within-named Company
with full power of substitution in the premises.

Dated,_____

NASSAU LIFE INSURANCE CO. *Cynthia A. Francis*
   In presence of
BY *Vak Greene*

NOTICE. THE SIGNATURE TO THIS ASSIGNMENT MUST CORRESPOND WITH THE NAME AS WRITTEN UPON THE FACE OF THE CERTIFICATE IN EVERY PARTICULAR, WITHOUT ALTERATION OR ENLARGEMENT, OR ANY CHANGE WHATEVER.

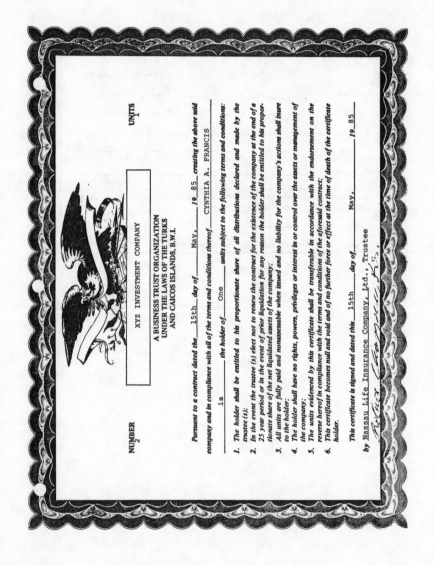

NUMBER

XYZ INVESTMENT COMPANY

A BUSINESS TRUST ORGANIZATION
UNDER THE LAWS OF THE TURKS
AND CAICOS ISLANDS, B.W.I.

UNITS

Pursuant to a contract dated the 15th *day of* May, 19 85 *creating the above said company and in compliance with all of the terms and conditions thereof* CYNTHIA A. FRANCIS *is* the holder of One *units subject to the following terms and conditions:*

1. *The holder shall be entitled to his proportionate share of all distributions declared and made by the trustee (s);*

2. *In the event the trustee (s) elect not to renew the contract for the existence of the company at the end of a 25 year period or in the event of prior liquidation for any reason the holder shall be entitled to his proportionate share of the net liquidated assets of the company;*

3. *All units are fully paid and nonassessable when issued and no liability for the company's actions shall inure to the holder;*

4. *The holder shall have no rights, powers, privileges or interest in or control over the assets or management of the company;*

5. *The units evidenced by this certificate shall be transferable in accordance with the endorsement on the reverse hereof in compliance with the terms and conditions of the aforesaid contract;*

6. *This certificate becomes null and void and of no further force or effect at the time of death of the certificate holder.*

This certificate is signed and dated this 15th *day of* May, 19 85

by Nassau Life Insurance Company, Ltd., Trustee

NUMBER
3

UNITS
49½

XYZ INVESTMENT COMPANY

A BUSINESS TRUST ORGANIZATION
UNDER THE LAWS OF THE TURKS
AND CAICOS ISLANDS, B.W.I.

Pursuant to a contract dated the ___15th___ day of ___May,___ 19_85_ creating the above said company and in compliance with all of the terms and conditions thereof ___JOHN H. DOE___

is _____ the holder of $ One-Half _____ units subject to the following terms and conditions:

Forty-Nine

1. The holder shall be entitled to his proportionate share of all distributions declared and made by the trustee(s);

2. In the event the trustee(s) elect not to renew the contract for the existence of the company at the end of a 25 year period or in the event of prior liquidation for any reason the holder shall be entitled to his proportionate share of the net liquidated assets of the company;

3. All units are fully paid and nonassessable when issued and no liability for the company's actions shall inure to the holder;

4. The holder shall have no rights, powers, privileges or interest in or control over the assets or management of the company;

5. The units evidenced by this certificate shall be transferable in accordance with the endorsement on the reverse hereof in compliance with the terms and conditions of the aforesaid contract;

6. This certificate becomes null and void and of no further force or effect at the time of death of the certificate holder.

This certificate is signed and dated this ___15th___ day of ___May,___ 19_85_

by _Nassau Life Insurance Company, Ltd.,_ Trustee

NUMBER
4

XYZ INVESTMENT COMPANY

A BUSINESS TRUST ORGANIZATION
UNDER THE LAWS OF THE TURKS
AND CAICOS ISLANDS, B.W.I.

UNITS
49½

Pursuant to a contract dated the 15th day of May,   19 85 creating the above said
company and in compliance with all of the terms and conditions thereof   JANE E. DOE
      is   the holder of& One-Half units subject to the following terms and conditions:
Forty-Nine

1. The holder shall be entitled to his proportionate share of all distributions declared and made by the
   trustee (s);

2. In the event the trustee (s) elect not to renew the contract for the existence of the company at the end of a
   25 year period or in the event of prior liquidation for any reason the holder shall be entitled to his proportionate share of the net liquidated assets of the company;

3. All units are fully paid and nonassessable when issued and no liability for the company's actions shall inure
   to the holder;

4. The holder shall have no rights, powers, privileges or interest in or control over the assets or management of
   the company;

5. The units evidenced by this certificate shall be transferable in accordance with the endorsement on the
   reverse hereof in compliance with the terms and conditions of the aforesaid contract;

6. This certificate becomes null and void and of no further force or effect at the time of death of the certificate
   holder.

This certificate is signed and dated this 15th day of   May,   19 85

by Nassau Life Insurance Company, Ltd., Trustee

NUMBER

UNITS

A BUSINESS TRUST ORGANIZATION
UNDER THE LAWS OF THE TURKS
AND CAICOS ISLANDS, B.W.I.

Pursuant to a contract dated the _____ day of _____ 19_____ creating the above said company and in compliance with all of the terms and conditions thereof _____ the holder of _____ units subject to the following terms and conditions:

1. *The holder shall be entitled to his proportionate share of all distributions declared and made by the trustee (s);*

2. *In the event the trustee (s) elect not to renew the contract for the existence of the company at the end of a 25 year period or in the event of prior liquidation for any reason the holder shall be entitled to his proportionate share of the net liquidated assets of the company;*

3. *All units are fully paid and nonassessable when issued and no liability for the company's actions shall inure to the holder;*

4. *The holder shall have no rights, powers, privileges or interest in or control over the assets or management of the company;*

5. *The units evidenced by this certificate shall be transferable in accordance with the endorsement on the reverse hereof in compliance with the terms and conditions of the aforesaid contract;*

6. *This certificate becomes null and void and of no further force or effect at the time of death of the certificate holder.*

This certificate is signed and dated this _____ day of _____ 19 _____

by _____

IN WITNESS WHEREOF, the CREATOR, TRUSTEE, EXCHANGOR, and CERTIFICATE HOLDER(s) have hereunto set their hands and seals in token and recognition of the conveyance, delivery, and acceptance of the property and the obligations and the duties herein assigned and hereby agree and assent to all the stipulations as imposed on the pages of this indenture.

NASSAU LIFE INSURANCE COMPANY, LTD.

Watter R. Simons
CREATOR

By *Veronica D. Williams*
FIRST TRUSTEE
(Attorney-in-fact)

Cynthia A. Francis
EXCHANGOR

The undersigned *Robert E. Baskin* being an officer authorized by the laws of the Turks and Caicos Islands to administer oaths, does hereby certify that the above named CREATOR, TRUSTEE, and EXCHANGOR all personally appeared before me on this day in Grand Turk, Turks and Caicos Islands, B.W.I., on behalf of the CREATION of and for the ESTABLISHMENT of the following CONTRACTUAL BUSINESS TRUST ORGANIZATION:

XYZ INVESTMENT COMPANY

SUBSCRIBED AND SWORN to before me by the above signatures THIS FIFTEENTH DAY OF MAY, 1985

TO CERTIFY WHICH, witness my hand and seal of office.

Baskin Notary Public
OFFICIAL SIGNATURE

MINUTES

OF

XYZ INVESTMENT COMPANY

Nassau Life Insurance Company, Ltd., duly appointed Trustee of the above named Company, hereby declares this contract to be in full force and effect and, by the signature of its Trustee below, pledges best efforts on behalf of the Company.

Signed and Dated

MAY 15, 1985

By Nassau Life Insurance
    Company, Ltd.,
    Trustee

By _____

MINUTES

OF

XYZ INVESTMENT COMPANY

In conformity with paragraph seven (7) of this indenture for
the above named Company, the undersigned Trustee hereby accepts
fees and remuneration as agreed of Two Hundred Fifty Dollars
($250.00)   per year with payment to be paid in advance yearly.
The annual fee may be paid by this Company or by an affiliated or
subsidiary entity.

By Nassau Life Insurance Company,
Limited, Trustee

Signed and Dated
MAY 15, 1985

By _____

MINUTES

OF

XYZ INVESTMENT COMPANY

Nassau Life Insurance Company, Ltd., Trustee for the above named Company, hereby appoints:

<table>
<tr><td>JOHN J. DOE</td><td>and</td><td>JANE E. DOE</td></tr>
<tr><td>as President (Agent)</td><td></td><td>as Secretary (Agent)</td></tr>
</table>

of the above named Company on a non-exclusive basis.

Their duties shall be to operate the Company affairs and business matters on behalf of the Certificate Holders and Trustee of the Company, including the signing of checks, deeds, and other documents.

The said Agents shall be reimbursed for any expenses they may incur on behalf of the Company and by separate contract shall draw reasonable fees for their services.

By the signatures below, the above named Agent President and Agent Secretary hereby accept their appointment, together with the responsibilities pertaining thereto.

By Nassau Life Insurance Company,
Limited, Trustee

Signed and Dated

MAY 15, 1985

By _____

_____
President

_____
Secretary

MINUTES

OF

XYZ INVESTMENT COMPANY

The Trustee adopted the following resolution: The execution
of business and routine day-to-day matters not requiring a Trustee Minute may be carried out as convenient by the Trustee,
Agent President, or Agent Secretary.

The Agent President or Agent Secretary should inquire of the
Trustee for guidance in proper handling of important matters
before proceeding.

                              By Nassau Life Insurance Company,
                                 Limited, Trustee
Signed and Dated

MAY 15, 1985

                              By _____

                                 _____
                                 President

                                 _____
                                 Secretary

MINUTES

OF

XYZ INVESTMENT COMPANY

The Trustee, Nassau Life Insurance Company, Ltd., was approached by Cynthia A. Francis, the Exchangor and sole owner of Certificate Number one (1) for one hundred (100) Capital Units of this Company, with her proposal to sell ninety nine (99) units of her total one hundred (100) units. Her offer was accepted by the Trustee and the sale is evidenced by the attached Bill of Sale.

Cynthia A. Francis also proposed to grant an indefinite and irrevocable option of sale of her remaining one (1) Capital Unit of this Company for the sum of Ten Dollars ($10.00). This option was accepted by the Trustee with no action taken to exercise the option at this time.

By   Nassau Life Insurance Company,
         Limited, Trustee

Signed and Dated

MAY 15, 1985

By   *Robert Chappell,*

MINUTES

OF

XYZ INVESTMENT COMPANY

Nassau Life Insurance Company, Ltd., Trustee of the above named Company, proposed to the following:

JOHN J. DOE   and   JANE E. DOE
President (Agent)   Secretary (Agent)

that they each acquire a Certificate for forty nine and one-half (49-1/2) Capital Units now held by the above Company. The Trustee offered to exchange One Dollar ($1.00) and both Certificates, each for forty nine and one-half (49-1/2) Capital Units of the above named Company, for certain real or personal property, to wit: the sum of One Hundred Dollars ($100.00) and other items of value as listed on Schedules A and B hereof. It was agreed by the parties hereto that this was neither a gift nor a sale. The offer was accepted and the exchange consummated.

Signed and Dated

MAY 15, 1985

By   Nassau Life Insurance Company
     Limited, Trustee

By   _Robert E. Chappell, Jr.,_

     _____
     President (Agent)

     _____
     Secretary (Agent)

MINUTES

OF

XYZ INVESTMENT COMPANY

Nassau Life Insurance Company, Ltd., as Trustee of the above named Company, herein accepts the directive that in the event the undersigned Agent President and/or Agent Secretary resigns, becomes incapacitated, or dies, the successor Agent President and Agent Secretary shall be as follows:

Agent President: Agent Secretary:

First_____   First_____

Second_____   Second_____

Third_____   Third_____

Fourth_____   Fourth_____

By Nassau Life Insurance Company, Ltd.
Trustee

Signed and Dated

MAY 15, 1985   By _____

                             _____
                             President

                             _____
                             Secretary

MINUTES

OF

XYZ INVESTMENT COMPANY

Nassau Life Insurance Company, Ltd., as Trustee of the above named Company, herein accepts the directive that upon the death of the Certificate Holders, the Units of Certificates are to be reissued as follows:

Name: Units:

_____   _____

_____   _____

_____   _____

_____   _____

_____   _____

By Nassau Life Insurance Company, Ltd.
Trustee

Signed and Dated

MAY 15, 1985   By _Robert Chappell Jr._

_____   _____
President

_____
Secretary

FINANCIAL INSTITUTION MINUTE

OF

XYZ INVESTMENT COMPANY

It is resolved by the Nassau Life Insurance Company, Ltd., Trustee of the above named Company, that the cash exchanged into this Company as designated in paragraph six (6) of this indenture and subsequent receipts shall be deposited in the following financial institution:

_____

located at _____

This account, at the election of the President Agent or Secretary Agent, can be a Checking, Savings, or Certificate of Deposit Account. The authorized signatures shall be:

<table>
<tr><td>JOHN J. DOE
President (Agent)</td><td>and</td><td>JANE E. DOE
Secretary (Agent)</td></tr>
</table>

Either signature shall be required for checks, withdrawals, or transfers. Any and all documents required by the above said institution for the opening of said account are hereby authorized and incorporated into this Minute.

Authorized and agreed by the undersigned Trustee, on this FIFTEENTH DAY OF MAY, 1985.

By   Nassau Life Insurance Company,
      Limited, Trustee

By   *Robert Chappell*

      _____
      President

      _____
      Secretary

MINUTES

OF

XYZ INVESTMENT COMPANY

Nassau Life Insurance Company, Ltd., by the power vested in it as Trustee of the above named Company, hereby appoints:

JOHN J. DOE and JANE E. DOE

as First Contingent Trustees to act as full Trustees upon the death, incapacity, or the resignation of the undersigned Trustee.

By Nassau Life Insurance Company
Limited, Trustee

Signed and Dated

MAY 15, 1985

By _____

President _____

Secretary _____

MINUTES

OF

XYZ INVESTMENT COMPANY

XYZ INVESTMENT COMPANY

SCHEDULE A

List all Real Property on this Schedule

SCHEDULE B

Received $100.00
Paid out $ 99.00
Received $100.00

List all Property other than Real Property on this Schedule

Chapter XI

Common Business and Legal Forms with Instructions

In previous chapters we discussed the various tax benefits which may be derived through utilization of the Contractual Company. We will now explore the various legal forms utilized by the trustee of the companies to realize those benefits. Concise instructions describing the specific use of each form follow, along with a generic copy of each instrument.

Assignment

Similar to a Bill of Sale, an Assignment transfers the intangible rights of one property owner (Assignor) to another (the Assignee). Since an Assignment is the relinquishment or transfer of a valuable right from one person to another, it is subject to many of the legal requirements of Deeds to real estate and Bills of Sale. Under an Assignment, the Assignee obtains only those property rights that the Assignor has and nothing more.

The general form below will suffice to assign property rights of almost any description. In attempting to execute the form a person would fill in the appropriate blanks on the form.

ASSIGNMENT
General Form

For Value Received I _____, of
_____ Street, City of _____,
State of _____, hereby assign, transfer, and set
over to _____, of _____ Avenue,
City of _____, State of _____,
all my right and title and interest in a certain agreement dated
_____, 19_____, by and between
_____ and _____
subject to all the terms and conditions thereof and hereby remise,
release and quit claim unto_____,
all my right, title and interest in and to the said property.

Dated _____, 19____. _____

Bill of Sale

Bills of Sale are utilized to transfer personal (as distinguished from real) property of a *tangible* (rather than intangible) nature. Note that the Grantor's name appears first, and the city, county, and state of his residence must also be provided. The consideration (money paid in exchange for the property being transferred) is then provided along with the name of the Grantee (party receiving the property and paying the money).

Since the Grantor transfers the property, in exchange for money consideration, the Grantee does the opposite.

Below you will find a sample Bill of Sale form. You should fill in the blanks following the instructions by inserting the appropriate name(s), amount(s) of money to be paid, or description of the property(s).

BILL OF SALE (ABSOLUTE)
General Form

KNOW ALL MEN BY THESE PRESENTS, That I, _____ of the city of _____, in the County of _____ and the State of_____, in consideration of_____Dollars ($_____), lawful money of the United States, to me paid by _____ of _____, the receipt whereof is hereby acknowledged, do hereby grant, bargain, sell, transfer and deliver unto _____ the following goods and chattels:

(Itemize)

TO HAVE AND TO HOLD all and singular the goods and chattels to _____ and his executors, administrators, assigns to their own use forever.

And I hereby covenant with the grantee that I am the lawful owner of said goods and chattels; that they are free from all encumbrances; that I have good right to sell the same as aforesaid; and that I will warrant and defend the same against the lawful claims and demands of all persons whomsoever.

IN WITNESS WHEREOF, I,_____, hereunto set my hand, this _____day of_____, 19_____.

Signed, sealed and delivered
in the presence of us:

_____   _____(Seal)

_____   _____(Seal)

Common Law Trust

Often called a business trust, or Massachusetts Trust, the Common Law Trust is an unincorporated association managed by Trustees for the benefit of its Certificate Holders.

The Common Law Trust is formed through execution of a written declaration of trust. The purposes of the Trust, along with the powers of the Trustees, are often listed in a trust indenture which accompanies the Trust Declaration.

The common characteristics of a Common Law Trust, created under the right of contract, are the free transferability of its shares, the continuity of its existence, the limited liability of its Trustees, and centralization of management. None of these characteristics have been held essential to create this form of trust, however.

The extent to which the Certificate Holders take part in governing or managing the business of the Common Law Trust is an important consideration in considering the limited liability of the Certificate Holders.

ESTABLISHMENT OF A BUSINESS TRUST

1. *Declaration of Trust*. Made on _____,
19,_____ by _____
_____ [*insert
names of five individuals*] as Trustees and _____
_____ (stockholders).

2. *Purpose.* The purpose of this Trust is that the Trustees shall hold and manage properly the earnings, the proceeds of which will be divided into shares whose certificates are to be held by the shareholders.

3. *Name.* This Trust is to be named _____
Company Unincorporated. It shall conduct all business under this name.

4. *Term of Office.* Of the five Trustees _____
_____, and _____

will hold office until the first annual meeting of stockholders.
_____ and _____
will hold office until the second annual meeting of stockholders.

Should a Trustee prove unable to fulfill his term of office, the remaining Trustees shall fill the vacancy for the unexpired term.

5. *Election of Trustees.* The Trustees are to be elected by the stockholders. Three are to be elected at the first annual meeting and two are to be elected at the second annual meeting. The election of Trustees shall follow this same pattern in alternative years thereafter.

6. *Trust Property.* Trust property is to be held by the Trustees in joint tenancy, with survivorship among the remaining Trustees upon the death, resignation, or removal of any of them.

The Trustees hold legal title to all property belonging to the Trust and have absolute control thereof.

7. *Powers.* The Trustees may engage in any business, including sale, exportation, manufacture, production, purchase, or transportation of _____
[describe nature of Business Trust]. The Trustees may enter into any contracts necessary to conduct the business, lend and borrow money, indemnify each other, and employ counsel and initiate suits at law, equity or arbitration _____
_____ *[List other powers.]*

8. *Officers.* The Trustees will elect annually a President, Vice-President, Treasurer, and Secretary from their ranks. These Officers will have the authority and perform the duties usually incident to officers in a corporation. The Secretary shall keep a record of all stockholder, Trustee, and Officer's meetings.

9. *Certificates.* The beneficial interest in the Business Trust shall be held by the shareholders in the form of Certificates having a par value of $_____ (dollars).These are to be considered personal property to be passed on in such manner upon the death of a stockholder.

10. *Duration.* This Trust shall continue for a term of ____ years, at which time the then Trustees shall wind up its affairs, liquidate its assets, and distribute them among the stockholders.

11. *Compensation.* The Trustees are to be compensated as follows:_____

_____

_____

12. *Amendments.* The stockholders may amend this Declaration of Trust by a two-thirds vote, at an annual or special meeting. However, the clause that Trustees, Officers, employees and stockholders are exempt from personal liability may not be amended.

_____

_____

_____

_____

Signatures of Trustees

Deed of Trust

A Deed of Trust is an instrument used in many areas of the country as a mortgage. Under this document the Title to the property is placed in escrow with a third party (the Trustee under the Deed of Trust) who holds it until the obligation described in the Deed of Trust is satisfied. Usually this involves the creation of a debt upon the purchase of the property. Title is conveyed to the third party Trustee under the Deed of Trust which provides that he (the Trustee) will reconvey the property to the Grantor (the purchaser) upon full payment of the purchase price. The Debt is usually evidenced by a special form of Promissory Note called a Deed of Trust Note or Real Estate Lien Note.

When the debt secured by the Deed of Trust is satisfied the third party trustee delivers the Deed of Trust to the purchaser, or executes a Release of Lien, freeing him of any further obligations under the Deed of Trust.

A common, short form Deed of Trust is included which is valid in those states allowing utilization of the Deed of Trust with private right of Sale vested in the named Trustee.

DEED IN TRUST

THIS INDENTURE WITNESSETH, That the Grantor of the County of _____ and State of _____ for and in consideration of _____ Dollars, and other good and valuable considerations in hand paid, Convey_____and Quit Claim_____unto the _____ _____, a corporation of _____, as Trustee under the provisions of a trust agreement dated the _____ day of _____, 19_____, known as Trust Number_____, the following described real estate in the County of_____and State of _____, to-wit:

(Insert legal description here.)

TO HAVE AND TO HOLD the said premises with the appurtenances upon the trusts and for the uses and purposes herein and in said trust agreement set forth.

Full power and authority is hereby granted to said trustee to improve, manage, protect and subdivide said premises or any part thereof, to dedicate parks, streets, highways or alleys and to vacate any subdivision or part thereof, and to resubdivide said property as often as desired, to contract to sell, to grant options to purchase, to sell on any terms, to convey either with or without consideration, to convey said premises or any part thereof to a successor or successors in trust and to grant to such successor or successors in trust all of the title, estate, powers and authorities vested in said trustee, to donate, to dedicate, to mortgage, pledge or otherwise encumber said property, or any part thereof, to lease said property, or any part thereof, from time to time, in possession or reversion, by leases to commence in praesenti or futuro, and upon any terms and for any period or periods of time, not exceeding in the case of any single demise the term of 198 years, and to renew or extend leases upon any terms and for any period or periods of time and to amend, change or modify leases and the terms and provisions thereof at any time or times hereafter, to contract to make leases and to grant options to lease and options to renew leases and options to purchase the whole or any part of the reversion and to contract respecting the manner of fixing the amount of present or future rentals, to partition or to exchange said property, or any part thereof, for other real or personal property, to grant easements or charges of any kind, to release, convey or assign any right, title or interest in or about or easement appurtenant to said premises or any part thereof, and to deal with said property and every part thereof in all other ways and for such other considerations as it would be lawful for any person owning the same to deal with the same, whether similar to or different from the ways above specified, at any time or times hereafter.

In no case shall any party dealing with said trustee in relation to said premises, or to whom said premises or any part thereof shall be conveyed, contracted to be sold, leased or mortgaged by said trustee, be obliged to see the application of any purchase money, rent, or money borrowed or advanced on said premises, or be obliged to see that the terms of this trust have been complied with, or be obliged to inquire into the necessity or expediency of any act of said trustee, or be obliged or privileged to inquire into any of the terms of said trust agreement; and every deed, trust deed, mortgage, lease or other instrument executed by said trustee in relation to said real estate shall be conclusive evidence in favor of every person relying upon or claiming under any such conveyance, lease or other instrument, (a) that at the time of the delivery thereof the trust created by this indenture and by said trust agreement was in full force and effect, (b) that such conveyance or other instrument was executed in accordance with the trusts, conditions and limitations contained in this indenture and in said trust agreement or in some amendment thereof and binding upon all beneficiaries thereunder, (c) that said trustee was duly authorized and empowered to execute and deliver every such deed, trust deed, lease, mortgage or other instrument and (d) if the conveyance is made to a successor or successors in trust, that such successor or successors in trust have been properly appointed and are fully vested with all the title, estate, rights, powers, authorities, duties and obligations of its, his or their predecessor in trust.

The interest of each and every beneficiary hereunder and of all persons claiming under them or any of them shall be only in the earnings, avails and proceeds arising from the sale or other disposition of said real estate, and such interest is hereby declared to be personal property, and no beneficiary hereunder shall have any title or interest, legal or equitable, in or to said real estate as such, but only an interest in the earnings, avails and proceeds thereof as aforesaid.

If the title to any of the above lands is now or hereafter registered, the Registrar of Titles is hereby directed not to register or note in the certificate of title or duplicate thereof, or memorial, the words "in trust", or "upon condition", or "with limitations", or words of similar import, in accordance with the statute in such case made and provided.

And the said grantor_____hereby expressly waive_____ and release_____any and all right or benefit under and by virtue of any and all statutes of the State of _____, providing for the exemption of homesteads from sale on execution or otherwise.

In Witness Whereof, the grantor_____aforesaid ha_____ hereunto set _____ hand_____and seal_____this _____ day of _____, 19_____.

_____(Seal)   _____(Seal)
_____(Seal)   _____(Seal)
_____I,_____

State of_____ ⎫
                          ⎬ SS.
County of _____ ⎭

a Notary Public in and for said County, in the state aforesaid, do hereby certify that _____

_____
_____

personally known to me to be the same

person _____whose name _____ subscribed to the foregoing instrument, appeared before me this day in person and acknowledged that _____ signed, sealed and delivered the said instrument as _____ free and voluntary act, for the uses and purposes therein set forth, including the release and waiver of the right of homestead.

Given under my hand and notarial seal this_____day of _____, 19_____.

_____
Notary Public

For information only insert street address of above described property.

Grantor Trust

Under this Trust the Grantor(s) (party[s] transferring appreciated property into the Trust for the benefit of specific named beneficiaries) retains so much control over the use or enjoyment of the property transferred that, for tax purposes, he is deemed the owner. This generic term derives from the provisions of Section 671 - 678 of the Internal Revenue Code. It is significant mainly in the federal income and estate and gift tax realm.

The retention of control by the Grantor of the trust results in imposition of taxes on earnings from the property on his (the Grantor's) taxable estate and *not* the taxable estate of the named beneficiaries.

Lease

A lease is a special form of contract concerning land under which the Lessor (party giving lease rights) gives the Lessee (party receiving lease rights) the right of temporary use or occupancy of land and, sometimes, the right to erect improvements upon it. Due to the Statute of Frauds in effect in most states, leases involving land or which cannot be performed in a period of one year should be in writing. The actual term of a lease can be quite long—leases of ninety-nine years or more have been upheld in the courts.

The form below includes the essentials of a basic lease and will be valid in most states.

LEASES

a.   (DATE)

This lease agreement entered into this _____ day of _____, A.D. 19_____,

b.   (PARTIES)

by and between _____ hereinafter referred to as the Lessor and _____ hereinafter referred to as the Lessee.

c.   (DESCRIPTION OF THE DEMISED PREMISES)

Witnesseth that in consideration of the rental below specified and of the covenants hereinafter stipulated, the Lessor agrees to lease the following described premises situated at No. ____ _____ Avenue, _____ City, _____ County, State of _____, legally described as:

(Here include full legal description)

d.   (TERM)

To have and to hold the demised premises unto the lessee,

his successors and assigns for the term of _____ years, commencing the _____ day of _____, A.D., 19_____ and ending the _____ day of _____, A.D., 19_____.

e.   (RENT)

The rent for the term of this lease is $_____, payable without demand or notice in equal monthly installments of $_____ on the _____ day of each and every month of the term hereof beginning on the _____ day of _____, A.D., 19_____. Receipt is hereby acknowledged by the Lessor of the first month's rental in advance and $_____ as security deposit.

f.   (USE)

The use of the premises shall be for_____ _____ and for no other purpose except with the written consent of the Lessor.

g.   (ASSIGNMENT)

The Lessee may not assign this lease or to sublet any part of said premises without the written consent of the Lessor.

h.   (LESSOR'S MAINTENANCE RESPONSIBILITIES)

The Lessor hereby agrees to keep the entire exterior portion of the premises in good repair and maintenance. The Lessee shall give written notice to the Lessor of necessary repairs and the Lessor shall have a reasonable time to make same.

i.   (LESSEE'S MAINTENANCE RESPONSIBILITIES)

The Lessee agrees to maintain the interior portion of the premises in good repair at all times. However, alterations, additions or structural improvements made to the premises must have the written consent of the Lessor. Said alterations, additions or structural improvements shall remain a part of the premises at the conclusion of the term of this lease.

j.   (INSURANCE)

The Lessee agrees to carry adequate public liability insurance with a bona fide insurance company maintaining sufficient protections against any injuries or damages sustained by individuals while upon the demised premises for which the Lessor and Lessee may become liable.

k.   (DEFAULT REMEDIES)

The said Lessee hereby convenants and agrees that if a default shall be made in the payment of rent or if the Lessee shall violate any of the covenants of this lease, then said Lessee shall become a tenant at sufference, hereby waiving all right of notice, and the Lessor shall be entitled immediately to re-enter and retake possession of the demised premises.

l.   (TERMINATION)

The Lessee agrees to quit and deliver up said premises at end of said term in good condition as they are now, ordinary wear and tear excepted.

m.   (OPTION)

The Lessee has the option to renew this lease for a further term of _____ years beginning _____ and ending _____ for a total rental of $_____ payable $_____ per month. All other terms and conditions of this lease agreement shall remain in full force and effect.

n.   (QUIET ENJOYMENT)

As long as the Lessee performs all of the covenants and conditions of this lease and abides by the rules and regulations he shall have peaceful and quiet enjoyment of the demised premises for the term of this lease.

o.   (SIGNATURES AND WITNESSES)

In witness whereof, the Lessor and Lessee have executed this lease the day and year first above written.
Witness:

_____   By_____
                                       Lessor

_____   By_____
                                       Lessee
_____

Mortgages

Under a mortgage, the Mortgagor (party granting or giving the mortgage) pledges his/her property as security for

the repayment of a debt or for the performance of an obligation to the Mortgagee (party receiving the pledge of security
or performance). There are two distinct theories in the
United States concerning the effect of a mortgage. Under
the majority rule the holder of a mortgage has a mere lien
on the property pledged and holds no interest in the title
as a result.[1] In a minority of states, the holder of a mortgage
has actual legal title to the property.[2] In these states the mortgage acts as a deed conveying the entire estate to the lender
(Mortgagee). The conveyance becomes void upon satisfaction of the terms of the mortgage (repayment in full).

Due to difficulties and expense in "strict" foreclosure
(through legal action in the courts) Deeds of Trust, which
have been covered previously in this chapter, have been
utilized in many states and take the place, in many instances,
of outright mortgages, which are now falling into disuse.

The various divisions of a sample mortgage form follow.

MORTGAGE

a. (DATE)
THIS INDENTURE, made and entered into this _____
day of _____, in the year of our Lord
One Thousand Nine Hundred and _____.
b. (PARTIES)

---

[1]Lien theory states include: Alaska, Arizona, California, Colorado,
Florida, Georgia, Hawaii, Idaho, Indiana, Iowa, Kansas, Kentucky,
Louisiana, Michigan, Minnesota, Montana, Nebraska, Nevada, New
Mexico, New York, North Dakota, Oklahoma, Oregon, South Carolina,
South Dakota, Texas, Utah, Washington, Wisconsin, and Wyoming.

[2]Title theory states include: Alabama, Arkansas, Connecticut,
Delaware, Illinois, Maine, Maryland, Massachusetts, Mississippi,
Missouri, New Hampshire, New Jersey, North Carolina, Ohio,
Pennsylvania, Rhode Island, Tennessee, Vermont, Virginia, and West
Virginia.

BETWEEN _____, hereinafter called the
Mortgagor, which term as used in every instance shall include
Mortgagor's heirs, executors, administrators, successors, legal
representatives and assigns, and shall denote the singular and/or
plural and the masculine and/or feminine and natural and/or
artificial persons whenever and wherever the context so requires
or admits, party of the first part, and _____
hereinafter called the Mortgagee, which term as used in every
instance shall include Mortgagee's heirs, executors,
administrators, successors, legal representatives and assigns and
shall denote the singular and/or plural and the masculine and/or
feminine and natural and/or artificial persons whenever and
wherever the context so requires or admits, party of the second
part;

   c. (AMOUNT OF INDEBTEDNESS, INTEREST RATE,
      MANNER OF PAYMENT)
   WHEREAS, the said Mortgagor is justly indebted to the said
Mortgagee in the aggregate sum of_____
Dollars, lawful money of the United States, for money actually
loaned to the Mortgagor, with interest thereon to be computed
from the_____day of _____, 19_____,
at the rate of _____% per annum, and to be paid
_____
_____
according to a certain bond, note or obligation bearing even date
herewith.

   d. (DESCRIPTION OF PROPERTY)
   The Mortgagor hereby mortgages to the Mortgagee, ALL that
certain

(Here include description)

   e. (CONVEYANCE OF PROPERTY[3])
   NOW, THEREFORE, for and in consideration of the sum of

_____

[3]This paragraph can be omitted in lien theory states.

one dollar in hand paid by the Mortgagee, receipt whereof by the Mortgagor is hereby acknowledged, and also for the better securing of the payment of the said sum of money and interest thereon, and for the better securing of the performance of the covenants and agreements hereinafter contained, the said Mortgagor has granted, bargained, sold and conveyed, and by these presents does grant, bargain, sell and convey unto the said Mortgagee, that certain lot, piece or parcel of land above described.

f. (SIGNED, SEALED, WITNESSED)

IN WITNESS WHEREOF, the Mortgagor on the day and year first written, has executed these presents under seal.

In Presence Of:

_____   _____

_____   _____

                                _____

g. (ACKNOWLEDGED OF MORTGAGE)

State of _____)
                           } ss
County of _____)

I, an officer authorized to take acknowledgments according to the laws of the State of_____, duly qualified and acting, HEREBY CERTIFY that_____ to me personally known, this day personally appeared and acknowledged before me that_____executed the foregoing Mortgage, and I further certify that I know the said person(s) making said acknowledgement to be the individual(s) described in and who executed the said Mortgage.

Promissory Note

A Promissory Note is a written promise to pay which acknowledges the existence of a debt and spells out the terms and conditions for repayment. Under this instrument the Promissor (party making payments) agrees to pay the Promissee (the party receiving the payments) at a given rate of interest and over a period of time, specifically described by the note's terms.

While some notes are negotiable (freely transferrable to parties not named in the instrument), others are not. A note need not be negotiable for it to be considered valid.

PROMISSORY NOTE
General Form

$_____ City of _____, State of _____Date _____

FOR VALUE RECEIVED, I (or we, jointly, jointly and sever-ally) promise to pay to the order of _____
the principal sum of _____dollars
($_____) in lawful money of the United States, with interest thereon from _____ at the rate of_____% per annum until paid, payable on _____ and _____ thereafter, and if not paid as it becomes due, to be added to the principal and become a part thereof and to bear interest at the same rate.

_____ (Seal)

_____ (Seal)

Quit Claim Deed

Under this form of Deed the Grantor conveys only the right, title, and interest, which he owns at the time of convey-ance. The Grantee receives no warranties under this Deed. This sort of Deed is a favorite of the Internal Revenue Serv-ice and is utilized to pass title at IRS sales of property after seizure for satisfaction of federal income taxes. The buyer (Grantee) receives no warranty or promises concerning the title under such a Deed.

QUIT CLAIM DEED
Individual or Corporation

THIS DEED, made the _____ day of
_____, 19_____, BETWEEN
_____ of No._____ _____
Street, City of _____, State of _____,
party of the first part, and _____ of
No._____ _____ Avenue, City of
_____, State of _____,
party of the second part.

WITNESSETH, that the party of the first part, in consideration of $_____, lawful money of the United
States, paid by the party of the second part, does hereby remise,
release and quitclaim unto the party of the second part, the heirs,
successors and assigns of the party of the second part forever.

ALL that certain plot, piece or parcel of land, with the buildings
and improvements thereon erected, situate, lying and being in the

(Here include legal description)

TOGETHER with all right, title and interest, if any, of the party
of the first part in and to any streets and roads abutting the above
described premises to the center lines thereof; together with the
appurtenances and all the estate and rights of the party of the
first part in and to said premises.

TO HAVE AND TO HOLD the premises herein granted unto
the party of the second part, the heirs or successors and assigns
of the party of the second part forever.

IN WITNESS WHEREOF, the party of the first part has duly
executed this deed the day and year first above written.

In Presence of: _____
                                        Grantor

_____

Warranty Deeds

These instruments convey real estate from the Grantor (party holding title) to the Grantee (party receiving title) in exchange for money, or other form of consideration.

Under the Warranty Deed the Grantor warrants (promises) that he holds title which will pass to the Grantee, in exchange for the consideration paid. Warranty Deeds may take various forms. For instance, a Special Warranty Deed limits the above guarantee of title to all claims against the property occurring *after* the original Grantor took title. Modification of the warranties under such a Deed will result in a change in deed nomenclature to reflect the lessor warranties (promises) being made by the Grantor to the Grantee, concerning the property to be deeded. Thus, we have the term "Special Warranty Deed" and "General Warranty Deed."

The short form Warranty Deed contained in the example below is sufficient, in most states, to transfer title and contains six specific warranties (covenants) guaranteeing the title. In many states, the inclusion of these specific written covenants would be superfluous since the law *implies* they are contained in the Deed and construes the instrument as if they were included, whether or not they are.

WARRANTY DEED
Statutory Short Form Full Covenants—Individual

THIS INDENTURE, made in the City of _____, State of _____, on the _____ day of _____, nineteen hundred and _____

BETWEEN _____, party of the first part and _____, party of the second part.

WITNESSETH, that the party of the first part, in consideration of _____ dollars, lawful money of the United States, paid by the party of the second part, does hereby grant and release unto the party of the second part, his heirs and assigns forever,

ALL that certain plot, piece or parcel of land

(Insert legal description)

together with the buildings and improvements thereon and all the estate and rights of the party of the first part in and to said property.

TO HAVE AND TO HOLD the premises herein granted unto the party of the second part, his heirs and assigns forever,

And the party of the first part covenants as follows:

FIRST—That the party of the first part is seized of the said premises in fee simple, and has good right to convey the same.

SECOND—That the party of the second part shall quietly enjoy the said premises.

THIRD—That the premises are free of encumbrances.

FOURTH—That the party of the first part will execute or procure any further necessary assurances of the title to said premises.

FIFTH—That the party of the first part will forever warrant the title to said premises.

SIXTH—THE GRANTOR, in compliance with Section 1 - 3 of the Lien Law of the State of _____, covenants that the grantor will receive the consideration for this conveyance and will hold the right to receive such consideration as a trust fund to be applied for the purpose of paying the cost of the improvement before using any part of the total of the same for any other purpose.

IN WITNESS WHEREOF, the party of the first part has hereunto set his hand and seal the day and year above written. In presence of:

_____ (Seal)

Chapter XII

Nassau Life and Its Products

Nassau Life Insurance Company, Ltd. was incorporated in the Turks and Caicos Islands on January 20, 1978, not only for the purpose of acting as trustee for offshore companies, but also for providing a wide range of products for protection and savings or investment.

As I have pointed out earlier, we have been witnessing the breaking down of our major institutions in America and the collapse of a 50-year-old economy that is being replaced by a new economy. What we need to do is to get into the new economy as soon as possible. One of the ways we can do that is through what I call the modern application of the ancient truth of transcendence. I go back to the 18th century German philosopher Kant, who gave us the science of transcendence, or what came to be known as *Kantianism*. This is the ability to transcend the limits of common thought. We have a serious problem in the United States today, and the only way for the average American taxpayer to deal with it, in my opinion, is to transcend the problem—*to transcend the limits of common thought.*

What I have done is to formulate ways in which the U.S. citizen can legally transcend the monumental labyrinth of bureaucratic rules and regulations that have made it just about impossible for the average citizen and small business person to function within the repressive system created by

his own government—a system created, of course, or so we
are told, for our own welfare and protection. Consider, for
example, the rules and regulations of the Securities and Exchange Commission which restrict the raising of capital to
the point where if you could accomplish it, the risks are too
great. It's nonproductive by the time you go through the
elaborate routine that you must follow in order to register
an issuance and make sure that every word is exactly right
in the prospectus. Most experts in securities will tell you that
there is no way under the sun that you could end up with
a perfect prospectus. There is always some way that the government can say, "Now wouldn't this be clearer if you said
it another way." And even if it's the high-paid lawyer who's
preparing the prospectus, it's the guy who's trying to start
a new business venture who runs the risk of being told he's
just broken the law and may have to go to jail. The stated
purpose of the SEC was "to monitor the integrity of the
capital markets." Did the SEC maintain the integrity—or
destroy the market?

Actually, it doesn't even matter if the business is a success
or a failure. If the government, for whatever reason, wants
to put a company out of business, it will find ways to do
it. If you think your government is there to protect you,
the citizen, think again. The government of the U.S. can
act only through its agents. Many of its agents are young
attorneys who would kill their grandmothers or put someone
out of business in order to get their names in the newspapers.

It has always been my opinion, for instance, that the IRS
and the Securities and Exchange Commission are the real
muscle of the Federal Reserve Bank. Any bank could call
and say, "Hey, we're having problems here. These mutual
funds are taking away our deposits." Savings and loans
could do the same. They could see that their deposits were
decreasing, rather than increasing, month by month. They
would want some action by the Securities and Exchange
Commission to keep the money in the banks, or in the sav-
s and loans, if the venture capitalists, or those engaged

in the sale of securities, were causing funds to go somewhere else besides into banking and savings and loan institutions.

Historic Changes in the Banking Industry

Perhaps a short history in U.S. economics will help to shed light on our current predicament. Part of the problem originated in 1934 when investment banking and commercial banking were divided. In all of Europe, and also in South America, investment banking and commercial are still one and the same. But in the United States in 1934, investment banking (stock brokerage firms) and commercial banking were divided. They were not to commingle, although the investment banks financed their portfolios through the commercial banks. All the investment banks would do is take their confirmations down and hand them to the bank and the bank would monetize that immediately and credit it to their account and they would charge interest. So there was a good relationship between the investment banking people and the commercial banks.

From about 1965, under the Lyndon Johnson administration, to about 1978, during the Jimmy Carter administration, the commercial banks had everything going their way. They had it all. Then you saw the advent under Carter of the money market fund. I think Carter and Ronald Reagan are probably aligned with the same people because the commercial banks seemed to have it all for a long period of time, and then you saw the gigantic growth of the money market funds. That was the investment bankers' way of saying, "Look, you rascals, we're going to do the same thing that you're doing and we're going to take some of that power, and a lot of that money, away from you." And indeed they forced the commercial banks into some very, very difficult times, as witnessed by the greatest number of bank failures since the Depression. Hundreds of billions of dollars were going into the money market funds.

Business Investment Economy

Another point needs to be made here to further explain our evolution in the U.S. from the old economy to the new economy. America had always been a business investment economy. Then, with the advent of Ralph Nader, we had a radical change. Ralph Nader was a tool used at that time to change the business investment economy to a consumer economy—an economy, you might say, designed to protect us from ourselves. The emphasis went away from business investment, where the emphasis had traditionally been in our supposedly free enterprise system.

You had probably heard, as I had from the time I was a child trying to earn spending money selling products, delivering newspapers, and doing odd jobs, that you could incorporate anything. You could sell shares, you could raise capital for a business idea and you could do anything within the law to make that idea work. If you worked real hard and were real smart, you might even get rich with your idea. That's pretty much the way it was until 1965, and the way it had been throughout the country's economic history. But in 1965 the Great Society tightened the screws down with the Securities and Exchange Commission and made it extremely difficult to pursue that old-fashioned, all-American concept of building a better mousetrap to catch a better business return.

And when the Great Society's consumer economy took hold, with its necessity for regulations which required more tax, coupled with roaring inflation through the 1970s, the average American's discretionary income—a factor too often overlooked in its importance to the economy—disappeared. When that happened, the wheels came off the U.S. economy and it has continued in a tailspin toward what I believe will be the ultimate demise of the economy and our major institutions as we have known them.

Thus, in about 1972, the new economy (or underground

economy) commenced to evolve out of necessity. Barter associations, commodity banks, exchange groups, thousands of private schools and tax reform groups sprang up all across the nation.

Transcending the Problem

The point of all this is that there are deep problems within the structure of the American economy—but the average person has no way, no freedom, of doing something about these problems within the system. This is where I call on the philosophy of Kant and the science of transcendence. We transcend the problem. And the system of transcendence that we use is the nonresident alien Business Trust Organization, or the Contractual Company.

We begin by forming an association: International Society of Independent Business Administrators. Once you're a member of ISIBA you can buy an offshore trust company. This is the freedom of association provided for in the U.S. Constitution: we have the right to associate in any lawful manner. If we wanted to get together and form a communist party in the U.S., we have the right to do so. And we certainly have the right to form ISIBA, which could have its headquarters in Switzerland, Germany, England or anywhere we want those headquarters to be. For our purposes, we want ISIBA headquarters to be in the Turks and Caicos Islands.

The next step is the formation of a Contractual Company. I have explained how this is done in Chapter X. Once you have formed a Contractual Company, you can purchase what we call the SAFE Deposit Account.

The SAFE (Swiss American Financial Exchange) Deposit Account is only sold to Contractual Companies. Nassau Life Insurance Company, Ltd., the trustee for those Contractual Companies, does not do business in the United States. That is important. The U.S. tax code says that a company can have information offices, and therefore information officers, in the U.S. (it can also have warehouses) and not be effectively connected with U.S. trade or commerce. If it were effectively connected, the company would be required to file tax returns.

Swiss banks, for example, operate the same way in this matter as Nassau Life Insurance Company, Ltd. A Swiss bank might have an information office in San Francisco, for instance, and if you walked in and said, "I want to open a Swiss bank account," you would not be allowed to do that. Well, not *exactly*. The information officers at the Swiss bank in San Francisco would tell you something like this, "Well, we can give you all the information, but the account would have to be opened in Switzerland." And then they would begin giving you the information you would need to open such an account, and they would say, "Here's the form. We'll help you fill out the form for opening the account. Now what amount did you think you wanted to deposit? Okay, fine, give us the check for that amount and we'll mail that for you, along with the form opening the account."

Voila! You have just walked into a Swiss bank in downtown San Francisco and for all practical purposes opened a Swiss bank account. But legally, you have opened the account in Switzerland, where you mailed the necessary forms, and all the Swiss bank in San Francisco did was assist you as an information officer. That's accepted. But you can't open a Swiss bank in downtown San Francisco and put up a big sign saying, "Open Your Swiss Bank Account Here!" And Nassau Life Insurance Company, Ltd. can't open an office anywhere in the U.S. and sell insurance. But we can maintain information offices throughout the U.S.

How does the SAFE Deposit Account transcend the problem of the Securities and Exchange Commission rules and regulations that have made it so difficult for the average person to operate within the U.S. economy? There is an exemption in the Securities Act for insurance policies. Insurance is exempt. It is not considered to be an investment contract. It is not considered to be a security if there is risk on behalf of the insurance company involved. Accumulation Fund Endorsement is attached to an insurance contract, so that all the funds placed in the contract accumulate and show interest. This is a whole life insurance policy. It is going to pay the death claim—whatever the policy stipulates as the figure to be paid upon the death of the insured Contractual Company officer. There is a small cost for the protection under a life insurance policy.

The Accumulation Fund Endorsement

But the important part of this contract is the Accumulation Fund Endorsement, and that makes it exactly like a money market fund, or similar to a deposit that one would make in a savings and loan or a savings account in a bank. Life insurance companies can do everything that a bank can do except offer checking accounts. (Actually, it could have draft accounts for clients, as Merrill Lynch has done with its money market fund, using what they call a ready cash fund.)

The financial end of the SAFE Deposit Account works this way: one unit of the SAFE Deposit Account would cost $1,200 per year plus $42 ISIBA membership fee. For the first year, $900 of that $1,200 covers the cost of the insurance; $300 is a contribution to the Accumulation Fund. Each year thereafter $300 goes into the insurance portion and $900 into the Accumulation Fund. That's for one unit. Any additional deposit that a person makes goes directly into the Accumulation Fund; no portion of the additional deposit goes into the insurance. Even the $300 going to insurance is not all cost since the policy accumulates cash volume.

The Accumulation Fund is like a demand account: it can

be withdrawn at any time. There is a penalty for early withdrawal before ten years of five percent of the amount withdrawn, but on any additional deposits over and above that $1,200 annual deposit, there is no penalty for withdrawal.

A SAFE Deposit Account can be a ten-year plan, twenty-year plan, or a continuing one. It is designed to be a private security plan in lieu of social security. The Accumulation Fund might be used for college expenses, business expansion, emergency cash, for whatever reason that might require cash. This money is readily available. The Accumulation Fund has consistently been paying 13 percent interest. Although interest rates are coming down, we hope to maintain a high rate.

Variety of Benefits from Nassau Life Products

These are some of the benefits to be gained from using the various estate planning products of Nassau Life Insurance Company, Ltd.

Guaranteed Income Annuity—This is for the estate which looks for an income that will provide gifts or loans for the lifetime of its beneficiaries. The plan allows the estate to have more immediate income from funds previously invested in real estate, CDs, or stocks and bonds. The estate is relieved of the possibility of its beneficiaries outliving their cash reserves. Not only guarantees for five and ten years of income are provided, but also for the entire life of the first beneficiary of the estate. A one-time deposit is all that is required in order to start the income within 30 days, which will continue for life thereafter.

Flexible Deferred Annuity—This product is for the estate which would like to build a large cash sum, as it pleases. Deposits can be made into the account at any time, for any amount, with the idea of drawing a guaranteed monthly or annual income at a later date, when extra income is needed.

Educational Annuity—This product helps take care of the future educational needs of children or grandchildren. The plan provides for a one-time deposit and disbursements according to college needs of the recipient. The projected costs for attending a four-year state college in the year 2000 are $51,000; projected costs for attending a private college are $98,000. At the current interest rates, a deposit of just $9,000 at birth could provide for the necessary funds to attend the four-year state college.

Term to Age 100 Life Plan—This product is used by estates to pay off outstanding debts and final expenses. Coverage can be obtained up to age 85.

* * * * * * *

All of the aforementioned contracts are owned by the Contractual Company. All proceeds are made payable to the company. Writing the contracts in this manner accomplishes the following:

- Interest accumulates on a tax-deferred basis.
- Eliminates any estate or inheritance taxes on proceeds.
- Eliminates probate cost and provides complete privacy for those funds in the companies.
- Keeps the funds that are in the companies in the privacy of the family, thereby eliminating the need for third parties to be involved, such as bankers, lawyers or tax collectors.

CERTIFICATE OF MASTER CONTRACT ISSUED TO MEMBERS OF THE INTERNATIONAL SOCIETY OF SENIOR CITIZENS

SWISS AMERICAN FINANCIAL EXCHANGE
ASSURANCE COMPANY LIMITED
of
The British Crown Colony of the Turks & Caicos Islands, British West Indies

Certificate of SAFE DEPOSIT ACCOUNT
(hereinafter known as the "Certificate")

This certificate is issued, subject to the terms and conditions of the master contract issued to members in good standing of the International Societe of Senior Citizens.

In Consideration of the application, when received by the Home Office and a copy of which is attached hereto and made a part hereof, for this certificate and of the payment of premiums shown in the application. Swiss American Financial Exchange Assurance Company Limited will pay the sum insured hereunder to the Beneficiary immediately upon receipt of due proof that the death of each Insured that has occurred while this certificate is in force, subject to the provisions and conditions on this and the following pages.

The Amount of Insurance applicable to any named Insured shall be the amount shown for such named Insured in the application for this certificate.

Unless Changed as provided in this certificate, the beneficiary shall be as set out in the application.

ACCUMULATION FUND

This Certificate is issued with an agreement under which the Certificate Holder may deposit 5,000.00 annually commencing the first or second year. Lesser or greataer amounts will be accepted as per the attached Accumulation Fund Agreement.

This Certificate is issued in consideration of the application, a copy of which is attached to and made a part of this certificate, and the payment of deposits in accordance with the terms and conditions of this certificate.

THE CONDITIONS AND PROVISIONS on this and the following pages are part of the master contract.

SIGNED at the Home Office of the Company on the date of issue.

Secretary *Janet C Wright*   President *Robert Chappell*

Registrar

Delphine Simons and Associates

As agent officer of __XYZ INVESTMENT COMPANY__ I herewith request that you submit the following application for a S.A.F.E.(term to 100) Deposit Account with Swiss American Financial Exchange Assurance Company Ltd. The name of the officer to be covered is __JANE E. DOE__.

Application for S.A.F.E.(term to 100) Deposit Account with Swiss American Financial Exchange Assurance Co. Ltd.

1. (a) Name of proposed Insured (Print in full)
JANE   F.   DOE
First   Middle   Last

(b) Residence 214 N. MAIN ST.
CENTER CITY CA, 90021
Number and Street / City or Town / County / State / Zip

2. (a) Amount of deposit (b) Plan Initial Face Amount
T100 $ 25,000 $__
(c) Method of payment
☒ Annually ☐ Semi-Annually ☐ Quarterly ☐ Monthly

3. Has the first deposit been made?
Yes or No YES
If paid, state amount and how paid $_____

4. Pay benefits to (name of company).
XYZ INV. CO.

9. A. Is there any impairment now existing in your health or physical condition? If so, give full particulars. — NO
B. Have you ever had any chronic disease, or any illness or abnormal condition lasting more than one month? If so, give particulars. — NO
C. Have you consulted a physician at any time within the last five years? If so, give name and address of each physician consulted and full particulars as to illness or accident and result of treatment. — NO
D. Have you ever made application or been examined for insurance without obtaining the insurance as applied for? If so, give full particulars. — NO
E. Do you use any alcoholic stimulants or habit-forming drugs to excess? — NO
F. To be answered if applicant is a woman: Are you now pregnant? If so, how far advanced? — NO

5. (a) Date of Birth Age (b) Place of Birth U.S.A.
7 26 30   State or Country CA.
Month Day Year Town LOS ANGELES
(c) ☐ Single (d) ☐ Male (e) Height 5 ft. 4 in.
☒ Married ☐ Female (f) Weight 140 lbs.

6. (a) Occupation ACCOUNTANT
(b) Name and Address of Employer(s) SELF
(b) How long so engaged? 30 YRS.

7. Special Requests:
Effective Date OCT. 20, 1984
1st Renewal Date OCT 20, 1985
Excepted for Issuance on this 20th Day of May, 1985.
Robert Chappell, Pres.

8. If plan is participating, dividends are to be used as follows:
1. ☐ Paid in cash 2. ☒ Left on deposit

The above answers are complete and true.

12. Dated at GRAND TURK on Oct 19, 19 85
by John A. Blanco / Jane E. Doe
Information Officer / Signature of Applicant Officer

I, the undersigned and applicant, do hereby give the trustee of the International Societe of Senior Citizens my proxy to vote for any member and/or officer of the Board of Governors. This proxy shall be in force until specifically rescinded by me in writing and delivered to the trustee.

Signature

**CERTIFICATE OF MASTER CONTRACT ISSUED TO
MEMBERS OF THE INTERNATIONAL SOCIETE
OF INDEPENDENT BUSINESS ADMINISTRATORS**

Swiss American Financial Exchange
ASSURANCE COMPANY LIMITED
of
The British Crown Colony of the Turks & Caicos Islands, British West Indies

Certificate of SAFE DEPOSIT ACCOUNT
(hereinafter known as the "Certificate")

CERTIFICATE OWNER: ___XYZ Investment Company___   CERTIFICATE#: ___10496___

ON THE LIFE OF: ___John J. Doe___   AGE LAST BIRTHDAY: ___64___

DATE OF ISSUE: ___February 30, 1985___

INITIAL AMOUNT OF INSURANCE   : $ 20,000.00

ULTIMATE AMOUNT OF INSURANCE   : $ 10,000.00

FIRST YEAR DEPOSIT   : $ 2,400.00

FIRST YEAR ACCUMULATION FUND   : $ 600.00

RENEWAL DEPOSITS   : $ 3,000.00

    PERIOD PAYABL   :   Annually

    DUE DATE: February 30, 1986

BENEFICIARY
As named in the application unless amended.

This certificate is issued, subject to the terms and conditions of the master contract issued to members in good standing of the International Societe of Independent Business Administrators (hereinafter known "I.S.I.B.A.").

SWISS AMERICAN FINANCIAL EXCHANGE will pay to the Beneficiary the Initial Amount of Insurance to the Anniversary following Age 60; the ultimate amount thereafter, immediately upon receipt at the Home Office of the Company of due proof of death of the Certificate Holder while this certificate is in full force, and to provide the other Benefits, Rights and Privileges of this certificate.

ACCUMULATION FUND

This Certificate is issued with an agreement under which the Certificate Holder may deposit $___3,000.00___ annually commencing the first or second year. Lesser or greater amounts will be accepted as per the attached Accumulation Fund Agreement. This money will be held by the Company and accumulated at Compound interest at a rate of not less than 4% per annum.

This certificate is issued in consideration of the application, a copy of which is attached to and made a part of this certificate, and the payment of deposits in accordance with the terms and conditions of this certificate.

THE CONDITIONS AND PROVISIONS on this and the following pages are part of the master contract.

SIGNED at the Home Office of the Company on the date of issue.

THIS CERTIFICATE HAS NO RESTRICTIONS AS TO TRAVEL, RESIDENCE, OCCUPATION,
AVIATION, MILITARY OR NAVAL SERVICE IN TIME OF WAR OR PEACE.
ACCIDENTAL DEATH BENEFIT AND WAIVER OF PREMIUM
DISABILITY, IF APPLICABLE, EXCEPTED.

SECRETARY   PRESIDENT

FORM CF 1006   **PARTICIPATING CERTIFICATE**

SWISS AMERICAN FINANCIAL EXCHANGE ASSURANCE COMPANY LIMITED

ACCUMULATION FUND

The Company hereby agrees to accept deposits for the purpose of providing a Retirement Annuity to the Insured subject to the conditions stated in this agreement.

Deposits. While the certificate to which this agreement is attached, is in full force and effect and in a deposit paying status and there is no indebtedness thereon, the Insured may deposit sums of money in amounts acceptable to the Company. All deposits are payable to the Home Office of the Company and no deposits shall be a valid obligations of the Company unless the deposits are made directly to the Company.

Accumulation Fund. Such deposits shall be held by the Company with interest at not less than four percent per annum. The accumulated amount of such deposits is herein called the Accumulation Fund. Interest shall be credited as of each certificate anniversary on which there is a balance in the Accumulation Fund, and shall be based on the average balance of the Accumulation Fund during the certificate year ending on such anniversary, or the ending balance whichever is the lesser amount. Amounts previously accumulated may be deposited in this Accumulation Fund and if sufficient may be used to fund an annuity. In the event of death the interest shall be payable on the average balance to that date.

Retirement Annuity. On the Retirement Date, which is the anniversary of the certificate to which this rider is attached following the Insured's 65th birthday, the amount of the Deposit accumulated under this Agreement will be automatically applied to purchasing a monthly income for life, with ten years certain, payable to the Insured on the basis of the Company's Guaranteed Settlement Options contained in the certificate. By making written application the Insured may elect either an earlier or later Retirement Date providing that this latter Retirement Date is not beyond the anniversary of the policy nearest the Insured's 70th birthday.

Automatic Deposits Payments. The Company will at any time after funds have been deposited under this agreement and without further action of the Insured, pay from the Accumulation Fund a sum sufficient to cover any deposits thereafter becoming due under the certificate and remaining unpaid on the last day of grace, not withstanding the fact that the Automatic Deposit Loan provision of the certificate might otherwise be effective. Such deposit shall include the deposits for any Supplemental Agreements attached to the certificate. It is provided, however, that if the amount available in the Accumulation Fund be not sufficient to cover such deposits, the Company shall apply the amount available to the payment of a lesser deposit installment, any remainder insufficient to cover a full installment, regardless of amount, will be used to provide one additional monthly deposit.

Settlement. If the certificate, to which this rider is attached, is surrendered, or if it becomes a death claim, the amount of deposits made under this provision and remaining to the credit of the Accumulation Fund together with interest thereon as above provided, shall be refunded. The Accumulation Fund may be used together with the cash value of the certificate to which this rider is attached for an election of settlement options as stated in the certificate at any time.

Right of Withdrawal. The Insured shall have the right, upon due written request made to the Company, to withdraw all or any part of the Accumulation Fund. The Company shall reserve the right to defer the granting of any cash withdrawal, except when made to pay a deposit on a certificate or certificates issued by it, for up to six (6) months after application therefor is made. Any cash withdrawal during the first ten (10) years shall have a charge of 5% on the amount withdrawn. The Accumulation Fund may be used, without charge, to pay deposits for the certificate to which this rider is attached.

Application of Certificate Provisions. All provisions of the certificate not inconsistent with any of the provisions of this agreement shall apply to this Agreement to the same extent as if incorporated herein at length.

IN WITNESS WHEREOF. The Swiss American Financial Exchange Assurance Company Limited has caused this Agreement to be executed at The British Crown Colony of the Turks Caicos Islands, British West Indies.

SECRETARY   PRESIDENT

Nassau Life Insurance Company, Ltd. executive quarters in Nassau, capital of the Bahamas.

Nassau Life Insurance Company, Ltd. 'The Evolving Institution'

Nassau Life's home office is strategically located in the Turks and Caicos Islands, the British crown colony approximately 335 miles southeast of Nassau (575 miles from Miami), with regularly scheduled flights from both Miami and Nassau. In Chapter V, I made it clear why the Turks and Caicos Islands is an advantageous jurisdiction for forming offshore companies: *It is the best tax haven jurisdiction in the world.*

Rock Sound Club Tax Planning Seminars

A unique addition to the facilities owned by Nassau Life Insurance Company, Ltd. is the internationally famous Rock Sound Club on the beautiful Bahamian island of Eleuthera, 72 miles from Nassau. Eleuthera Island was the first landing place of the original settlers of the Bahamas in 1648. They took the name of their new home from the Greek word *eleutheria,* meaning "freedom." I find this is a particularly apt name because this is precisely the objective being pursued by Nassau Life on behalf of individual American taxpayers- —*freedom.*

The Rock Sound Club on Eleuthera is now the site of regular seminars conducted by Nassau Life experts in estate tax planning. The seminars offer comprehensive analysis of the uses of tax haven jurisdictions in reducing tax liabilities, including detailed presentations on the formation of Contractual Companies for individual U.S. taxpayers. Insights on economic history and ways to survive under the new economy are also given in unique video specials such as the highly acclaimed "Free to Choose" series by Nobel laureate Milton Friedman and commentaries by Dr. Richard Armey, former head of the North Texas State Economics Department who is now a U.S. congressman.

The Rock Sound Club resort was originally the private

Guests of Nassau Life's secluded Rock Sound Club resort on the lovely island of Eleuthera enjoy some of the most gorgeous, and least crowded, white sandy beaches in the Bahamas. The island is also famous for its spectacular scuba diving and snorkeling, reef and bone fishing and a wide variety of recreational and historical attractions.

Tax savings and estate planning seminars are conducted in the tropical luxury of the internationally famous Rock Sound Club on the beautiful Bahamaian island of Eleuthera.

estate of Arthur Vining Davis, the founder of the Aluminum Corporation of America (ALCOA). The spacious Rock Sound Club cottages are nestled quietly among groves of palm trees and guests can enjoy sunny, balmy weather throughout the year. Resort amenities include an Olympic-sized swimming pool, tennis courts and fine dining. Eleuthera's long, wide, sandy beaches are among the most gorgeous—and least crowded—in the Bahamas. Eleuthera is also noted for spectacular scuba diving and snorkeling, reef and bone fishing and a variety of resort, recreational and historical attractions throughout the island.

Chapter XIII

Probate: Avoiding the High Cost of Dying

Robert Kennedy, when he was attorney general of the United States, called probate "a political toll booth exacting tribute from widows and orphans." New York's memorable reform mayor, Fiorello La Guardia, called the probate court "the most expensive undertaking establishment in the world." Despite the widespread criticism of the probate system that has intensified through the years, it remains a dangerous threat to the assets that a person may have acquired through a lifetime of hard work.

Death and inheritance taxes are also an attempt on the part of government to redistribute wealth in the misguided belief that it will benefit society as a whole. As Milton Friedman said, "Trying to do good with other people's money *simply has not worked.*" Friedman effectively exposes the fallacy of trying to achieve some form of equality by penalizing, upon their death, people who have managed to accumulate important assets during their lifetime. Says the Nobel laureate economist:

> Much of the moral fervor behind the drive for equality comes from the widespread belief that it is not fair that some children should have a great advantage over others simply because they happened to have wealthy parents. Of course it's not

fair, but is there any distinction between the inheritance of property and the inheritance of what at first sight looks very different: inherited talent? Some youngsters have inherited wealth not in the form of bonds or stocks but in the form of talent. The inheritance of talent is no different from an ethical point of view than the inheritance of other forms of property, of bonds and stocks, of houses or of factories. Yet many people resent the one, but not the other.

If you want to give your child a special chance, there are different ways that you can do it. You can buy him an education, an education that will give him skills enabling him to earn a higher income. Or you can buy him a business. Or you can leave him property, the income from which will enable him to live better. Is there any ethical difference between these three ways of using your property? Or again, if the State leaves you any money to spend over and above taxes, should you be permitted to spend it on riotous living, *but not permitted to leave it to your children?*"[1]

If you expect to be an heir to any significant asset or sum of money, it would be a good idea to give a copy of this book to the relative or friend from whom you expect the inheritance. Any asset placed in a Contractual Company will avoid probate and death and inheritance taxes.

Proper planning by a person with assets to pass on to friends or relatives may save the friends and relatives a tremendous ordeal when he or she dies.

Two sons of a deceased mother said to me recently that they wished they had known about the problems of probate

---

[1]"Free to Choose: A Personal Statement," publicly televised documentary by Milton Friedman.

one year ago. They are attempting to pay $120,000 in cost, all of which could have been avoided had they known of our methods.

The Probate System and Its Hazards

An article in *Business Week* realistically appraised the problem concerning wills and probate. "Named in a will?" it asked. "It can take years for you to collect." The story continued:

> If you suddenly discover that you are the beneficiary of an estate, don't be too fast to order your yacht. These days it can take years for rightful heirs to collect their legacies. And legal and court costs, as well as taxes and debts, can sometimes shrink an estate to a pittance.
>
> Don't try to hasten things along by pressuring the executor or his attorney. No matter how efficient they are in assembling the assets of an estate, paying debts and taxes, and finally making disbursements, delays are inevitable. Dozens of claimants get a crack at the estate before you can collect a penny.
>
> Creditors have from four months to a year, depending on state law to make their claims. Then the federal and state governments take their slices. Within nine months of the testator's death, the executor is required to file federal estate tax forms. But the Internal Revenue Service can take another year to audit the return, and state tax agencies will take a few months before they, too, are satisfied.[2]

---

[2]*Business Week,* June 3, 1972.

Even though a great number of wills cause problems, many authorities warn against dying without a will. The state will take over your estate and distribute what's left to the heirs according to their own guidelines without a will. Your spouse doesn't automatically get all of your estate. In some states, one-half to two-thirds of a person's estate is divided among surviving children. And if you haven't any children, your brothers, sisters, parents, even distant blood relatives could qualify for a share. Furthermore, your wife has to pay for an administrator, appointed by the court, to wind up your financial affairs, and a guardian to protect the rights of minor children. Even if she is named guardian, your wife still must post bond, another expense, and make periodic accounts to the court for the estate.

Even though a valid will is used, there is no guarantee that the wishes of the deceased will be carried out in a reasonable length of time or ever. Extreme situations keep us aware of the possible pitfalls that can affect our families at death.

Reader's Digest noted in an article titled, "The Mess in Our Probate Courts": "Inflated fees, paralyzing delays, patronage—these are only some of the many ugly abuses fostered by our antiquated and inefficient probate system." It continued:

> If the same new-model sedan were selling for $2,500 in one state and for only $225 a few states away, the automobile business would never be the same again. Yet, an important commodity that nearly every American family needs at least once—legal help in probating an estate—costs, according to the bar association's suggested scale of fees, a minimum of $400 in Gary, Indiana, and only $35 in York, Pennsylvania, barely 600 miles apart.
>
> This great spread in legal fees is only one of a number of faults, fumblings and frauds to be found in the American way of passing money and property from one generation to the next. The

high cost of dying is not the funeral: it's the legal
and administrative costs of getting the dead man's
estate—his lifetime earnings—through the probate
or surrogate courts. In some states they might be
called chancery or orphan's courts, but regardless
of the name, this legal institution, intended originally to help the average family, has become a
means of exacting an onerous ransom from the
bereaved.[3]

According to the same *Business Week* article, there are
other pitfalls to wills as well.

No matter how amicable the atmosphere may
appear among the heirs at the reading of a will,
don't be shocked if the will is later contested. The
challenger does not have to prove anything as sini-
ster as someone unduly influencing the deceased.
Little things like erasure marks, pencil notations,
unsigned amendments, or even unwitnessed
amendments on a will could make it invalid. One
legal expert alleges that 35 per cent of all wills are
broken.

The following story appeared in the *Dallas Times Herald*.[4]
A synopsis serves to illustrate how the will of a well-meaning
individual can cause unexpected hardship.

A woman named Billie Goff, 41, applied to go on welfare.
This is something she never anticipated. After all, she lived
in a handsome, well-furnished, two-story brick home.

Miss Goff inherited $428,609 from her stepfather with
whom she had lived since she was 3 years old. Nobody questioned the will's validity. However, at one point, Miss Goff

---

[3]*Reader's Digest,* October, 1966.
[4]*Dallas Times Herald,* October 3, 1965.

was down to 35 cents and a meager supply of groceries, with no hope of securing a job because of paralysis that affected her speech.

Why doesn't she have any money, considering the size of the estate? To begin with, her stepfather owed back income taxes amounting to about $40,000. A number of valuable notes could go back on the estate for payment if the other parties defaulted, even though they were backed up by property.

"[Unfortunately], it's possible that the estate won't be worth anything," said a probate judge.

The matter boiled down to this in the simplest form: any creditors must be taken care of by the estate according to the law because a person can't inherit something that belongs to someone else. What is baffling is that the estate is paying for a considerable number of things that in all likelihood do not mean the difference between eating and not eating for someone else. These include accountants who are determining the extent of tax liability and an attorney hired by the court to protect the interests of the estate. But still, there is not one penny for Billie Goff.

A similarly tragic story concerned an 80-year-old widow whose husband left a multimillion dollar estate and she never received a penny. Yet hundreds of thousands of dollars in payments to lawyers were approved by judges. The estate was mismanaged so deplorably that complaints were made to the President. Finally, a member of the board of governors of the American Bar Association declared the story such a dreadful example of judicial dereliction, it was impossible to find a sequel. But what financial comfort did those words provide the widow?

Handling Excess Procedural Baggage

An intelligent person with the ability to reason should by now realize that it is the complex set of statutory laws which has evolved in the United States that provides the basis for the legal and accounting professions. Their practitioners have studied years learning how to enrich themselves from the enforcement of those complex statutory laws and regulations. It is simply not in the best interest of the lawyer or accountant to face or even consider the possibility that a better way exists for handling tax and estate matters.

When an attorney is licensed to practice law, he becomes an officer of the court. This implies that he is actually working for the court. Sure the attorney is representing his client before the court—but in the manner which is in the best interest of himself and the court, i.e., in a manner actually prescribed by the court. The attorney could be subject to contempt of court charges if he represents the client's interest too strongly in a creative or unorthodox manner.

In recent years, accountants have been required to have a license to practice income tax accounting. An accountant cannot sign tax returns or charge a fee unless he has this license and follows the rules prescribed by the Internal Revenue Service. He may be subject to the assessment of a fine or penalty at the whim of the IRS. It therefore becomes clear that the accountant has been made the policeman for the IRS. It is not in the accountant's best financial interest or within the scope of possibility that he could actually look out for the client's best interest at the risk of sacrificing his own.

Thus one can expect very little assistance from his accountant or attorney in making estate and tax planning decisions since they are both, in a strong sense, agents for the enforcement of the government's statutory laws and rules.

Many people are not alone in this opinion, although few attorneys are willing to admit the facts because of self-interests involved. However, Chief Justice Warren E. Burger of the United States Supreme Court is one of the few legal professionals who has spoken out on the problem and indicated assignable causes. He told the *Los Angeles Times* in the mid-1970s some of his views concerning probate, including calling on the legal profession to reduce fees charged for probate, an area of the law that touches very directly upon the daily lives of most Americans.

Reminding attorneys of their pledge to "place the public interest ahead of private gain," Burger said the profession had allowed the "relatively simple" business of settling a will to "become encrusted with excess procedural baggage that...often adds unreasonably to the costs."

He later told the American Law Institute that legal costs could be cut if "American lawyers will put their ingenuity and inventiveness to work...to devise simpler methods than we now have."

Attorney Leo Kornfeld of New York wrote in *Money* magazine on the probate system. He made the following points:

1. Lawyers make their money handling estates, not planning them.
2. Fees for handling estates often bear no relationship to the amount of time spent by the lawyer on behalf of the estate. This is the real *racket* in probate.
3. It is a lot easier to exact an enormous fee from a dead man's estate than from a living client.
4. In the main, the handling of moderate estates is a cut-and-dried affair with much of the work done by the lawyer's secretary, and problems are solved by clerks at the probate court. Very little of the lawyer's own time is involved.
5. Very seldom does an attorney spend more than 15 to 20 hours of his own time handling a $100,000 estate. That is being generous.
6. Legal fees for relatively simple probate work have averaged out to over $1,000 an hour, in some instances. (Sixty dollars per hour is outrageous.)
7. Courts and bar associations rebuke lawyers

who try to change the deplorable system.[5]

Protecting Your Estate

A noted lawyer once said:

> You can have a will instead of a trust if you
> are willing to pay the price.

This may have happened to you: a friend or relative died and the estate was thrust into a time-consuming period known as probate in order to prove that the will was valid. This could have resulted in enormous inheritance taxes, high estate taxes, and large legal fees drastically reducing the estate. The Internal Revenue Service could have ruled adversely on stocks, paintings, antiques and other personal property.

When you pass on, your family may have to go through the same needless waste of time and money. As much as 30 to 50 per cent or more of your estate could be taken by taxes and fees. The financial security you promised your family might be destroyed when you die.

Now there is no need for your family to do without. You can legally avoid every dollar that your family may ever pay by learning a method that could save you many costs, including those for a will, an attorney, an executor and the additional burdens of inheritance, estate and gift taxes. This can be done in one simple process.

The method is a little known and rarely used instrument based on common law called the Contractual Company, which is similar to a pure trust system. It can be used by anyone with moderate or large assets who wants to save money for himself while he is alive and for his family upon his death.

---

[5]*Money,* January, 1973.

Compare Your Family Estate With Others

Since you have accumulated assets through your life, it is only right that when you pass on, your family should receive the full benefit and the full use of those assets. Proper tax and estate planning could keep those assets *intact* for the intended recipients, without a cent of probate or tax costs and without a moment of waiting.

The following are examples of small, medium and prominent family estates that were drastically reduced by premature debt payments, probate expenses and death taxes.

The first item to note in each sample is the gross estate. Subtract from this the premature debt payments which can cause severe hardships because even income-producing assets may have to be sold to meet debts. Normally, the income may have been used to make payments over a number of years. The resulting total equals the net estate.

However, the net estate is further reduced by further expenses comprising the sum of probate costs and death taxes. Probate expenses include administration costs, fees for the attorney, executor, consultant and appraiser, as well as commissions and losses from forced sale of properties. Death taxes encompass inheritance fees and obligatory payments to the government.

While some of these samples may seem startling, it is vital to note that the situation continues to worsen. No estate is safe from undue threats. Proper planning is the key.

The President

FRANKLIN DELANO ROOSEVELT
Residence, Hyde Park, New York

Gross Estate .... $ 1,940,999
Total Costs 574,867
Net Estate .... $ 1,366,132

SETTLEMENT COSTS

Premature Debt Payments .... $ 19,221
Probate Expenses 209,516
Death Taxes 346,130

Total Costs .... $ 574,867

Per Cent of Estate Lost 29%

Banker

CHARLES TEMPLETON CROCKER
Prominent Financier, San Francisco, California

Gross Estate .... $ 4,995,976
Total Costs 2,421,174
Net Estate .... $ 2,574,802

SETTLEMENT COSTS

Premature Debt Payments .... $ 48,680
Probate Expenses 136,037
Death Taxes 2,236,457

Total Costs .... $ 2,421,174

Per Cent of Estate Lost 48%

Accountant

ALWIN CHARLES ERNST
Senior Partner, Ernst & Ernst, Accountants
Cleveland, Ohio
(Died Intestate)

Gross Estate $12,642,431
Total Costs 7,124,112
Net Estate .... $ 5,518,319

SETTLEMENT COSTS

Premature Debt Payments .... $ 6,232
Probate Expenses 78,862
Death Taxes........................... 7,039,018

Total Costs .... $ 7,124,112

Per Cent of Estate Lost....................... 56%

Attorney

ALBERT PICARD
Prominent Attorney, San Francisco, California
(Died Intestate)

Gross Estate .... $ 1,003,599
Total Costs 486,737
Net Estate .... $ 516,862

SETTLEMENT COSTS

Premature Debt Payments .... $ 159,301
Probate Expenses 53,195
Death Taxes........................... 274,241

Total Costs .... $ 486,737

Per Cent of Estate Lost....................... 48%

Businessmen

GUY A. WAINWRIGHT

President, Diamond Chair Company
Indianapolis, Indiana

Gross Estate	$ 5,424,750
Total Costs	3,288,710
Net Estate	$ 2,136,040

SETTLEMENT COSTS

Premature Debt Payments	$ 25,020
Probate Expenses	89,520
Death Taxes	3,174,170
Total Costs	$ 3,288,710
Per Cent of Estate Lost	60%

EDWARD A. DEEDS

Chairman, National Cash Register Company
Dayton, Ohio

Gross Estate	$13,312,950
Total Costs	7,902,050
Net Estate	$ 5,410,900

SETTLEMENT COSTS

Premature Debt Payments	$ 234,260
Probate Expenses	139,490
Death Taxes	7,528,300
Total Costs	$ 7,902,050
Per Cent of Estate Lost	58%

ALBERT H. WIGGIN

Retired Chairman, Chase Manhattan Bank
New York, New York

Gross Estate	$20,493,990
Total Costs	14,865,310
Net Estate	$ 5,628,680

SETTLEMENT COSTS

Premature Debt Payments	$ 243,250
Probate Expenses	1,257,530
Death Taxes	13,364,530
Total Costs	$14,865,310
Per Cent of Estate Lost	72%

P. G. LAKE

Oil Operator, Tyler, Texas

Gross Estate	$ 3,541,940
Total Costs	1,471,510
Net Estate	$ 2,070,430

SETTLEMENT COSTS

Premature Debt Payments	$ 35,610
Probate Expenses	61,600
Death Taxes	1,374,300
Total Costs	$ 1,471,510
Per Cent of Estate Lost	40%

WINIFRED HILDERBRANDT

Widow, Oil Man, Oklahoma City, Oklahoma

Gross Estate .... $ 299,000
Total Costs   145,270
Net Estate .... $ 153,730

SETTLEMENT COSTS

Premature Debt Payments .... $ 56,170
Probate Expenses......................   21,840
Death Taxes...........................   67,260

Total Costs .... $ 145,270

Per Cent of Estate Lost...................... 36%

Columnist

HEDDA HOPPER

Newspaper Columnist, Hollywood, California

Gross Estate .... $ 427,660
Total Costs   165,970
Net Estate .... $ 261,690

SETTLEMENT COSTS

Premature Debt Payments .... $ 11,670
Probate Expenses......................   25,000
Death Taxes......................   129,300

Total Costs .... $ 165,970

Per Cent of Estate Lost...................... 37%

Architect

LUDWIG MIES VAN DER ROHE
Architect, Chicago, Illinois

Gross Estate	$	793,040
Total Costs		342,710
Net Estate	$	450,330

SETTLEMENT COSTS

Premature Debt Payments	$	24,250
Probate Expenses		107,670
Death Taxes		210,790
Total Costs	$	342,710
Per Cent of Estate Lost		41%

Chapter XIV

Legal Opinions Upholding The Contractual Company

The first legal opinion concerning the Contractual Company was not easy to obtain. I approached Michael Pinatelli, a tax specialist with the law firm of Bernard and Pinatelli in San Francisco. Michael was an intelligent and cautious young man.

After studying my methods, checking the cases and reviewing the applicable tax code sections, Michael Pinatelli was willing to write the limited, nontax opinion, only if he could go to the Turks and Caicos Islands. After the trip to Turks and Caicos, where he talked to attorneys, accountants and the attorney general of the Colony, Michael Pinatelli wrote the first legal opinion regarding the Contractual Company. After much research, Pinatelli stated, "The government will never be able to get a fraud penalty for the use of your system." A few days later he said, "I doubt that the government could even get a five percent negligence penalty." He seemed to become convinced of the merits of the system as time went on.

The following is Michael Pinatelli's legal opinion on the Contractual Company, dated December 5, 1979:

Attn: Mr. Robert Chappell

Re: Pure Business Trust Organizations

Dear Mr. Chappell:

After considerable research I am finally able to respond to your inquiries regarding the validity and non-tax advantages of a pure business trust organization.

A pure business trust organization is a form of business organization which has arisen out of the English Common Law. Smith v. Anderson (1880) L.R., 15 Chancery Division 247. Said entity is created by a contractual arrangement, most commonly referred to as a declaration of trust, whereby real and/or personal property is conveyed to trustees who hold and manage property for the benefit of certificate holders pursuant to the terms of the declaration of the trust.

An important note which must be made at this point is that it appears that the type of business trust organization created by the declaration of trust presented to this office differs in one major aspect from the most widely recognized form of business trust organization, the Massachusetts Business Trust. In a Massachusetts Business Trust there is a split in the title of the property held and managed by the trustees: the trustees hold the legal title but the certificate holders hold the equitable title. In the pure business trust organization created by the declaration of trust presented to this office the trustees hold both legal and equitable title; the only rights of the certificate holders are those given to them in the declaration of trust.

There is no question but that the type of pure business trust organization created by the declaration of trust used by Scientific Asset Management

Limited is recognized by the English Common Law (which Turks and Caicos follows) and it has been used successfully in the United States. Dunbar v. Brumfield (1930) 142 N.E. 148; see also 156 A.L.R. 67 for a sample copy of indentures similar in nature to the one used by Scientific Asset Management. Although I have been unable to find in California case law any case which deals with the particular type of pure business trust organization created by this type of declaration of trust, the California Supreme Court has officially sanctioned the use of a Massachusetts Business Trust in California and it appears that the reasoning pertaining to the validity of a Massachusetts Business Trust would be applicable to the pure business trust organization. Goldwater v. Oltman (1930) 210 Cal. 408. In fact, California now requires business trusts doing business in California to file a Statement of Designation by Foreign Association (filing fee $350.00). It is my opinion that any pure business trust organization which files such a statement when doing business in California increases its likelihood of receiving judicial approval if the issue as to its validity in California should ever arise.

The non-tax advantages of using a pure business trust organization are discussed in detail in Cavitch, Business Organizations, Vol. 3, Ch. 42, Matthew Bender (1971) and Ruhrlich, Organizing Corporate and Other Business Enterprises, 5th Edition, Matthew Bender (1975). My review of these works indicate there are five distinct benefits obtained from the use of a pure business trust organization; these are:

1) Continuity of existence;

2) Limited liability to the certificate holders;

3) Free transferability of interest;

4) Centralized management; and

5) Flexibility in creation and operation

Continuity of existence is provided for by the fact that the legal existence of the pure business trust organization is not terminated by the death or resignation of the trustee or trustees. The business organization continues with a successor trustee or trustees appointed pursuant to the provision of the declaration of trust. Nor does the death of any or all of the certificate holders terminate the existence of the business trust organization.

Limited liability of the certificate holders is an important characteristic in that it means that any liability incurred by the trustees on behalf of the business trust organization is limited to the extent of the assets held by the business trust organization. However, please note that there are two critical prerequisites which must be met in order for the courts to uphold the limited liability of the certificate holders. The first prerequisite is that the declaration of trust must specify that the certificate holders are not individually liable. The second prerequisite is that the certificate holders may not have any role in the operation and/or control of the business trust organization. This includes having no voice in the selection of trustees or their successors. (The declaration of trust shown to me by Scientific Asset Management Limited meets both prerequisites.)

Free transferability of interest means that the certificates may be sold, transferred, or traded by the certificate holders at their will.

Centralized management is brought about by the fact that the trustees and their agents are the sole managers of the business pursuits of the business trust organizations. Therefore, regardless of the number of certificate holders the operation of the business trust organization is tightly controlled.

Flexibility in creation and operation is obtained due to the fact that the trustees are limited in the conduct of the affairs of the business trust organization only as set forth in the declaration of trust. Normally, as is the case of the declaration of trust reviewed, the trustees are given great flexibility which enables them to adjust to changing market conditions and to take advantage of business opportunities as they arise.

As was agreed upon I have not discussed the internal workings of the pure business trust organization, nor the tax or securities aspect of their operation. All of the above holds true only if the pure business trust organizations are properly established and managed. It appears that the use of pure business trust organizations has been limited to a privileged few, therefore, there is a large area of legal uncertainty which surrounds their operation. However, with careful planning and operation the advantages of using a pure business organization may be substantial.

Sincerely,

Michael R. Pinatelli, Jr.
Attorney At Law

Second Legal Opinion

Joe Alfred Izen, Jr., a well known Houston attorney, came to the attention of Nassau Life Insurance Company, Ltd. because of his involvement in the appeal of the *U.S. vs. Dalstrom* case. His legal work in that case showed a certain brilliance as well as a knowledge of taxes, trusts and uses of offshore tax haven jurisdictions. In my opinion, Izen's briefs in the Dalstrom case contained the most convincing arguments of all the many briefs filed. The Ninth Circuit Court of Appeals reversed the lower courts convictions of all concerned. Many of the statements by the appeals court came directly from Izen's appeal briefs.

Izen is now under contract for his full-time services to Nassau Life Insurance Company, Ltd.

Legal opinions by Izen include the first one which was contracted for by Scientific Asset Management Co., Ltd., a subsidiary of Nassau Life Insurance Company, Ltd. The second opinion was written more recently and, until now, has never been distributed to anyone. The second opinion is the first comprehensive tax opinion written for the Contractual Company.

The following is the first legal opinion written by Joe Alfred Izen, Jr. and dated September 26, 1983:

Attn. Mr. Robert Chappell
Scientific Asset Management Co., Ltd.

Please consider this letter my formal opinion upon which you may rely for the purpose of responding to specific inquiries concerning the contractual trust companies utilized by estate and financial planners, both in your organization and others, for the preservation and accumulation of personal, family, and/or company financial estates.

Certain specific questions have been asked which I will address in their chronological order. The first question — Is a contractual company, such as those utilized by Scientific Asset Management, Ltd., a valid legal entity?

An examination of the contractual trust companies indicates that they are formed through the utilization of two basic documents. The first document is the Declaration of Trust under which a Trustee(s) receives property from a Creator(s) or Grantor(s) and contractually obligates himself, upon receipt of the property, to manage the property. The second document is the Trust Indenture. The trustee(s) accepting the property and undertaking to manage this corpus is contractually bound to follow, strictly, the specific terms of the Trust Indenture in carrying out his duties. Thus, the documents creating the Trust impose contractual obligations on the Trustee(s) to act as a Fiduciary with respect to the property and funds placed in his hands, initially, by the Creator(s) or Grantor(s). In my professional opinion these particular trusts, which are being utilized by SAM, are unquestionably valid legal entities arising out of the common-law and, more specifically, in this country, the Constitutional right to contract.

These contractual companies are often referred to as "pure" trusts. An explanation of their function, under the common-law of England, can be found in Smith v. Anderson, 15 Chancery Division 247 (1880). This Smith decision establishes the validity and viability of these contractual companies in English common-law jurisdictions beginning in 1880 and up to, and including, the present date. The Smith decision has never been reversed nor has its import been nullified through passing of negating statutes in the United Kingdom, or in any other common-law jurisdiction of the commonwealth, or otherwise. All of the various states of this country, save and except for the State of Louisiana, have founded their legal system on the common-law of England and have adopted its rule of "stare decisus" under which unwritten law is made through case law decisions. The State of California is no exception. Section 22.2 of the California Civil Code specifically adopts the common-law of England as the law of the state ". . .so far as it is not repugnant to or inconsistent with the Constitution of the United States or the Constitution or laws of this state. . . ."

Thus, it can be safely said that unless a specific statute or specific section of the Constitution of the State of California prohibits property ownership, or the carrying on of business by these entities, then they are indisputably valid.

The above statute adopting the common-law of England as the "rule of decision" in the State Courts of California, pre-dates the Smith decision and was enacted almost immediately upon the granting of statehood to the commonwealth of California. Contractual companies, such as those under consideration here, have been utilized, in this country, for hundreds of years and pre-date the American Revolution. The contractual company, acting through its Trustees to carry on active and on-going businesses, became popular at the turn of the century and continued in popularity until the decade of the Fifty's following World War II.

The Supreme Court of the State of California considered the legality and validity of this type of contractual company in Goldwater v. Oltman, 292 P. 624 (Supreme Court of California, 1930). In ruling in favor of the legality of the contractual arrangement the Supreme Court of California specifically noted, "Generally stated, a Trust of this nature is created wherever several persons transfer the legal title in property to Trustees, with complete power of management in such Trustees, free from the control of the Creators of the Trust, and the Trustees in their discretion pay over the profits of the enterprise to the Creators of the Trust or their successors in interest. *As thus defined it is apparent that such a trust is created by the act of the parties and does not depend on statutory law for its validity.* (See Goldwater at Page 327. Citing also Hecht v. Malley, 265 U.S. 144, 44 S.Ct. 462) The Supreme Court of California then stated, *"In the absence of controlling authority to the contrary, we can see no reason why such organizations with their limited liability should not be recognized in this state.* It is true that the statutes of this state provide for limited liability in the case of limited partnerships and corporations, but we find nothing in these statutory provisions that manifest an intent to limit the types of business organizations which shall enjoy this privilege to the two types of business organizations enumerated. Section 2220 of the Civil Code expressly states that trusts in personalty may be created for any purpose for which a contract may be lawfully made.... It seems clear to us that the settled legislative policy of this state is to lay no restrictions against the formation of trusts and personalty but rather to leave open to such organizations the conduct of any lawful enterprise. The law of trusts is just as much a part of the legislative policy of this state as the law of limited partnerships and corporations. It is true that trusts historically were not used for the purpose of running large business enterprises and were a development of the Equity Courts. The law, however, is not static, but is ever growing and expanding and in recent years this form of handling property has been extended to nearly every field of activity. *Just because a new use has been made of the trust does not mean that new principles of law are to be applied in determining the rights of the Trustees, cestuis que trust* (beneficiaries), *creditors of the trust or others that deal with the trust.*" See Gold-water at Page 629.

As stated before there has been no specific statute which has negated the viability of these contractual companies. Moreover, the regulatory efforts of the State of California have been consistent with the validity of these organizations. Section 25019 of the California Corporate Securities Law specifically includes "certificates of interest or participation in any profit-sharing agreement or collateral trust certificates" under its definition of security, and specifically excludes from the definition of security "any beneficial interest in any voluntary inter vivos trust *which is not created for the purpose of carrying on any business or solely for the purpose of voting, or any beneficial interest in any testamentary trust.*" The Trustees of the contractual company utilized by SAM are empowered to issue "Beneficial Interest Certificates" and to exchange these certificates for valuable property, which then goes into the corpus of the trust and is managed by the Trustees according to the terms of the trust indenture. The regulation of the issuance of the Beneficial Interest Certificates, under California Securities Law, is the strongest argument that can be made for the validity of these trust companies. If they were invalid the State of California would have nothing to regulate.

Much has been made of the distinction between those contractual companies wherein the holders of the Beneficial Interest Certificates own "equitable title" in the assets of the trust company and those contractual companies wherein the Trustees of the trust company own both legal and equitable title in fee simple, to the trust corpus, the holders of the Beneficial Interest Certificates having only the expectancy of sharing in any distribution of the trust corpus or profit *if* made in the sole discretion of the Trustees. The trust indenture utilized by SAM provides that the owners of the Beneficial Interest Certificates hold *no* legal or equitable title in the trust corpus or assets and, thus, the Trustees own title to all trust property in fee simple. This specific arrangement of ownership, in fee simple, of the assets of a trust company by the Trustees was specifically approved by the Supreme Court of the United States in Hemphill v. Orloff, 48 S.Ct. 577, 277 U.S. 537 (Supreme Court, 1928) wherein the Court, in examining the specific trust company at issue in that case, noted that the trust indenture of the trust company provided "Trustees shall hold the legal title to, and have the absolute and exclusive control of, all property at any time belonging to this trust subject only to the specific limitations herein contained. They shall have the absolute control management and disposition thereof.... Shareholder's meetings shall be held annually for the purpose of electing Trustees. *Interest in the estate shall be evidenced solely by certificates for participation shares, to be regarded as personal property*. The shareholder's death shall not operate to terminate the trust nor entitle the decedent's representative to an accounting or to take action in the Courts or elsewhere against the Trustees. *Shareholders shall have not title in*

the trust property or right to call for a Partition,
division or accounting." See Hemphill at Page
578.

Hemphill clearly validates fee simple ownership
of the trust property by the Trustees as provided
for in your trust indentures. When the Supreme
Court of the United States has ruled on an issue
its decision will be controlling, on interpretation
of common-law, and binding on the Supreme
Court of the State of California. Only in the event
a specific California statute is passed, in deroga-
tion of the common-law, could the arrangement
be invalidated. Since this has not occurred, this
form of ownership is viable and valid and not subject to statutory restriction.

The question has been asked — "Why do these
companies have the right to hold title to U.S.
property?" In the first place it must be noted that
the due process clause embodied in the Fifth
Amendment to the United States Constitution
allows aliens to own land in the United States subject only to reasonable restrictions by the various
states. There are no such restrictions in the State
of California which limit the right of foreign trust
companies to hold land in this State. A foreign
trust company organized in the Bahamas, or in
other English common-law jurisdictions, is a valid
legal entity in the country of its origin. As such,
unless restricted specifically by statute, it has the
right to hold property anywhere in the United
States. It should be further noted that the foreign
contractual companies stand on the same footing
as foreign corporations which have been gobbling
up U.S. lands with unprecedented and insatiable
appetite, both in the State of California, and in
others.

This does not mean that a contractual trust

company, carrying on a business in the State of California, or elsewhere, cannot be regulated by the state authorities. The Supreme Court of the United States, in the Hemphill decision, specifically addressed an attempt by the State of Michigan to regulate common-law trusts carrying on business within its borders and held in favor of reasonable regulation. (The trust company was required to obtain a Certificate of Authority to do business in the State of Michigan over its objection.)

The State of California requires foreign trust companies (either from foreign sister states or from English common-law jurisdictions) to file a statement and designation as a "foreign association" and pay a filing fee. However, "doing business in California" constitutes activity and conduct of ongoing commercial enterprise and the mere ownership of real property or personal property in this state would not constitute "doing business" under these rationales. An examination of California case law on this subject is replete with examples of ownership of real and personal property by contractual trust companies. Dunbar v. Redfield, 61 P.2d 744 (Supreme Court of California, 1936) and Siedletz v. Griffith, 114 P.2d 598 (Supreme Court of California, 1941) involved disputes arising out of ownership and management of mining claims and/or other mineral interests in the State of California. In both cases the ownership of the mineral interest by Trustees of the common-law trust companies was specifically noted and the Supreme Court disposed of the legal controversies presented to it in both cases in a manner consistent with the validity of such ownership. Also, in Alphonzo E. Bell Corporation v. Bellview Oil Syndicate, 116 P.2d 786 (Disctrict

Court of Appeal, 1st District, Division 2, California, 1941) an oil syndicate organized to develop and operate oil properties, and admitted by all parties to be a common-law trust, was held to be as business and thus sueable in its common name. See Alphonzo E. Bell Corporation at Page 790.

In Mary Pickford Company v. Bayly Brothers, Inc., 86 P.2d 102 (Supreme Court of California, 1939) the Supreme Court of California specifically noted the ownership of real estate by a common-law trust company and resolved the dispute before it in a manner consistent with such ownership. A thorough reading of the Mary Pickford Company case should dispell any doubt that a trust company has the capacity to own real estate in the State of California. In Bank of America National Trust & Savings Association v. Scully, 92 F.2d 97 (C.A. 10, 1937) the United States Court of Appeals for the 10th Circuit decided a similar dispute and recognized the right of a common-law trust company to purchase and sell real estate in that state.

The case law of other states is replete with examples of the utilization of contractual trust companies to take possession and ownership of land, to subdivide same, and then, ultimately, after management, to distribute the pro-rata share of profits, after sale and development, to the holders of the Beneficial Interest Certificates of the Trust.

None of the above Courts could have reached a decision on the merits had the trust companies lacked capacity of ownership in the real estate in question. Since the Trustee owned fee simple title (both legal and equitable) in the trust property they must execute all conveyances of real property in a manner consistent with the laws of the State of California and the Trust Indenture and/or other trust documents. As long as the strictures are complied with there is no question that the ownership and subsequent conveyance of property by these trust companies is legal and valid.

A person is "authorized to act for a trust company" as an agent or otherwise, in the same manner and under the same principles of agency as economic or legal representatives of a corporation, trust, partnership, limited partnership, or any other *recognized* legal entity which, under the terms of the law, is looked upon as a separate juristic person. The Trustees are empowered by the Trust Indenture to convey real estate. An execution of a deed by business trust company with acknowledgement by the executing Trustee(s) coupled with a specific minute of a meeting of the Board of Trustees authorizing such conveyance should, in all circumstances, be sufficient evidence of the authority to convey. I point out here that the Trustee(s) is empowered to convey property of the trust company "in the ordinary course of business" without specific approval and authorization obtained after a meeting of the Board of Trustees. The objection that the conveyance was made "out of the ordinary course of business" of the trust company is cured, under the terms of the Trust Indenture, through a specific meeting of the Board of Trustees. The holders of the Certificates of Beneficial Interest have no control over the actions of the Trustees and the Trustees have full and complete control to manage the trust corpus subject to the provisions and requirements of the "reasonable and prudent man" standards in the performance of their office. Furthermore, the Trustees may delegate all acts to be performed in the "ordinary course of business" to business managers or other executive personnel under the specific terms of the Trust Indenture. The Trustees have broad enough authority under the Indenture to authorize these excecutive employees and/or agents, such as business managers and directors, to convey real estate as long as the conveyance is specifically in the "ordinary course of business."

The business which can be carried on by a contractual company is as broad and far reaching as that of corporations or any other recognized legal entity. If an active ongoing business is carried out by the trust company through its Trustees, such as rendering of professional services, manufacturing, or any other activity other than the static holding of capital (such as real estate, bonds, etc.) for a profit, then the specific laws relating to qualification to "do business" in the state at issue must be consulted and complied with. Since the ownership of real estate does not qualify as "doing business" under most statutes, a title company need not concern itself with the other activities of the contractual company when issuing a Title Insurance Policy.

It has long since been decided that a corporation, such as Nassau Life Insurance Company, Ltd., may act as a fiduciary. Thus, the validity of its corporate services Trustee for many of the contractual companies organized by SAM cannot be seriously questioned. All doubts concerning the capacity of Nassau Life Insurance should be laid to rest through providing a copy of the Certificate of Incorporation and/or a Certificate in Good Standing of the Corporation from the appropriate Ministry in the Bahamas.

Lastly, I note that the validity and capacity of these contractual companies has been recognized in other "sister states" and would refer your attention, in this regard, to State v. Cosgrove, 210 P. 393 (Supreme Court of Idaho, 1922) and Pacific American Realty Trust v. Lonc Tot, 381 P.2d 123 (Supreme Court of Washington, 1963).

Note that this Opinion is being written specifically at the request of Scientific Asset Management, Ltd., and reflects representation of no other principal *other* than that organization. Should you need any further clarification of the somewhat exhaustive discussion of the principles outlined above please feel free to direct further correspondence.

Sincerely,

Joe Alfred Izen, Jr.
Attorney for Scientific
Asset Management Company, Ltd.

Latest Legal Opinion

In legal and accounting matters there are no absolutes. There are no guarantees. The most assuring thing that we can have is an opinion. Even when the Supreme Court rules on an issue brought before it, we still have only an opinion.

It is the opinion of the majority of the Supreme Court justices that forms the majority opinion—which is the law of the land until many years later when the same issue may come before the court for another opinion.

Following is Joe Alfred Izen, Jr.'s legal opinion, dated June 20, 1985, that is the first tax opinion ever written regarding Nassau Life's Contractual Company (Pinatelli's legal opinion was a nontax opinion):

Mr. Robert Chappell
Nassau Life Insurance Company, Ltd.
Nassau, The Bahamas

RE: (Requested Tax Opinion Letter—Addressing Tax Aspects of Contractual Trust Companies; Addressing the Broad Range of Tax Ramifications Realized From Use of Contractual Trust Companies in Income and Estate Planning for U.S. Citizens and Domestic Residents; Cataloging Unsuccessful Attacks by Internal Revenue Service on Trust Concepts Developed and Implemented by Nassau Life Insurance Limited.)

Dear Mr. Chappell:

You will recall my previous opinion letter of September 26, 1983, which has, apparently, stood the test of time. Although oft criticized and disparaged by various so-called "tax practitioners" throughout the United States, the opinions expressed therein along with the legal principles and authorities therein quoted, have yet to be shaken, either from direct onslaught by the Internal Revenue Service or by the "winds of legal change." Accordingly, the principles expressed therein are still sound and are incorporated by reference in the text of this opinion. A copy of the previous opinion letter should be attached to each disseminated copy of this text, both for the purposes of completeness and for full understanding of the views which I will now express.

Almost two years ago I undertook representation of your company, and its U.S. representatives, who were then facing the "awful onslaught" of the I.R.S., the very same investigation predicted by the "financial freedom consultant" W.

L. Comer, in his so-called laymen's opinion letter of April 23, 1983. Luckily, the "sour grapes" opinions expressed by Mr. Comer, trustee, in that letter, "have not stood the test of time."

As you know I briefed and personally argued the celebrated case of United States v. Dahlstrom, 713 F. 2d 1423 (C.A. 9, 1983) before the United States Court of Appeals for the Ninth Circuit. That Opinion, decided August 24, 1983, (not made part of the original opinion letter of September 26 of the same year) which dealt a death blow to I.R.S. hopes of utilizing mis-information schemes to terrorize average taxpayers with the spectre of criminal liability and deter them from engaging in creative tax planning. It is of great significance that the Solicitor General of the United States, the highest executive attorney in the land, tried but failed to reverse the teachings of Dahlstrom at the Supreme Court of the United States. But, even more significant than those efforts, was the Court of Appeals' cognizance of I.R.S. admissions which establish, beyond pall, the correctness of the entire thesis of the letter of September 26, 1983.:

"In support of its first contention, the Government argues that the law is clear that economic realities of a transaction rather than form are controlling for tax purposes. Consequently, the Government asserts that the Appellants were well aware of the inherent illegality of the tax deductions which flowed from use of the A.L.A. tax shelter program. The Government, however, has not pointed to any cases which invalidated the F.T.O.'s presented in this particular case. Moreover, the *Government's own expert*

> *witness, Karl K. Krogue, testified that the*
> *trusts created through implementation of the*
> *A.L.A. tax shelter program were valid legal*
> *entities."*

See Dahlstrom at P. 1427. The Dahlstrom trusts were inferior, tax-wise, to the contractual companies utilized by Nassau Life Insurance Company Limited. The Dahlstrom trust program emphasized that the *form* of the paper transaction would govern the substance and the trusts created lacked an adverse trustee which would prevent successful attack by the I.R.S. under the so-called "grantor trust provisions" of the Internal Revenue Code. (Section 671 through 679).

It is noteworthy that the Internal Revenue Service began its criminal investigation of Nassau Life Insurance Company and its principals, and agents, *prior* to the Court of Appeals decision in Dahlstrom and, although the "investigation" continued for almost a year thereafter, the United States Attorney was unable to prosecute.

Sadly, some elements of the I.R.S. believe that an all out seizure of "every shred of paper" will destroy a citizen's business. Its Agents act on these beliefs when they perceive it to be to their best advantage. I.R.S. abuses of Grand Jury secrecy, and Grand Jury procedures, have been well documented in other cases including Anderson v. U.S.; Criminal No. 83 - 010 and 83 - 031, United States District Court for the District of Wyoming and United States v. Kilpatrick. Yet, as long ago as 1923 the United States Court of Appeals, in examining and confirming the common law abhorrence of such conduct observed:

"The use of search warrants is confined to

cases of public prosecutions, instituted for
the suppression of crime or the detection and
punishment of criminals. In such cases their
legality has long been recognized as established on the grounds of public necessity."

See Agnello v. United States, 290 F. 671 (C.A.
2, 1923). The Agnello Court referenced several
decisions holding unconstitutional statutes that
authorized a Magistrate or Judicial Tribunal to
issue a search warrant which could be "...availed
of by individuals in the course of civil proceedings...." See Agnello at P. 678.

In September of 1984 I was called upon to
represent an information agent of Nassau Life
Insurance Company, Limited, who was villified
in the press as "marketing illegal trusts."

Although I entered the case expecting to defend
the validity of the trusts and the various ground-
work previously laid by the Dahlstrom decision
and my Grand Jury representation, this Government "challenge" never materialized. The I.R.S.
contented itself with claimed violations of Title
18 U.S.C. Section 371 and Title 26 U.S.C. Section
7206(2) against the two Defendants—charges
which did not address the validity of either the
trusts themselves or the tax planning associated
with them.

The final courtroom confrontation exposed the
perfidious nature of the I.R.S. campaign of lies
and mis-information. Through direct examination
the I.R.S. Special Agent Kevin Lafferty, the
Agent "in charge" of the Brownlee investigation,
we revealed that the claimed deductions on payments of interest to the trusts, by the U.S. citizens
he investigated, were at best for the Government,

a "gray area" and would not even support a criminal investigation under I.R.S. guidelines. A review of the attached excerpts of his testimony provides key insight into I.R.S. utilization of scare tactics, a very successful ploy in the Brownlee investigation—i.e. confront the trust promoter, or even taxpayer, with the "false certainty" that the trust is a sham and then extort a confession under false pretexts. (See Vol. I, PP. 74-85; Direct testimony of Agent Lafferty attached hereto and incorporated by reference in this opinion.)

Ultimately, the District Court instructed the jury that the trusts were legal entities and that the claimed deductions were valid, as long as the interest on the loans had been paid. (See Vol. I. P. 79, 80 and 81 and Vol. K, PP. 103-122.) That the District Court and the Government accepted the validity of the trust, and the claimed deductions, is conclusively proven by the Court's instructions to the jury, which constitute the Court's "Conclusions of Law" for the purposes of the criminal decision. That Traves V. Brownlee was thereafter acquitted of two felony counts of aiding and assisting in the preparation of fraudulent income tax returns, but convicted of conspiring to defraud the United States, by impeding the Internal Revenue Service, is of no precedence. The Court's instructions on the other hand, adopt the Ninth Circuit principles expressed in United States v. Dahlstrom for the Third Circuit and will forever frustrate the I.R.S. proliferation of distorted "tax propaganda" which has no legal or factual basis. It is this counsel's studied belief that as long as the principles expressed in this letter are strictly adhered to by the company and its representatives or associates, no criminal liability need be feared or even anticipated. See Traves V. Brownlee, Et

<u>Al, v. U.S.</u>, No. CR-84-52WKS, U.S. District Court, District of Delaware.

With the above ground rules established, I next turn my attention to the classification of the contractual trust company as an entity, for federal tax purposes. Historically, similar entities have been treated, under the federal income tax law, as trusts, corporations, or partnerships. Much of the case authority classifying this form of trust is of relatively ancient vintage but is still reliable. Ordinarily, in the past, a corporate "characteristics" test has been applied with the following distinctive criteria:

1. Associates.
2. Business objective.
3. Continuity of existence.
4. Centralization of management.
5. Limited liability for corporate debts.
6. Transferability of shares.

It has been stated that the decisive criteria in distinguishing a trust and a corporation are associates and business objective. Similarly, the distinguishing characteristics between a corporation and a partnership are centralization of management, continuity of existence, limited liability, and transferability of shares. See "Federal Taxation of the Business Trust," The Boston University Law Review," Vol. XL, No. 3, Summer, 1960.

While it has been stated that a Massachusetts Business Trust, *in its typical form* will "most frequently be taxed as a corporation under the federal income tax law," there is nothing typical about the form utilized by Nassau Life in comparison with the Massachusetts entity. Where the trust company lacks essential corporate indicia or characteristics, it will be taxed as a trust or partnership. See Pieroni Building Trust, 45 B.T.A. 157 (1941) and Sears v. Hassett, 45 F.Supp. 772 (B.Nass. 1942).

The frank admission, even in the case law, that a trust company can be classified, for tax purposes, as a trust, partnership, or corporation is hardly conducive to lucid tax planning. However, the trust company, as organized under the terms and provisions of the contract utilized by Nassau Life Insurance Company, does not "defy analysis" under these tests.

Since the holders of the beneficial interest certificates do not have, under the instrument, a right to participate in the decision making process with the trustees, there are no "associates" as contemplated by the Pieroni and Sears tests. The contractual company does have business objectives and these are spelled out in the trust indenture. There is no perpetual life consistent with the concept of "continuity of existence" endemic to a corporation. While there is centralization of management (a Board of Trustees or one Trustee) the units are not freely transferrable. Neither the trustee nor the holders of the units face individual liability for trust debts.

Based on the above tests, the contractual company cannot be classified as an association as it lacks "associates." The contractual companies cannot be classified as partnerships as, in many cases, only one trustee (Nassau Life Insurance Company, Limited) is chargeable with conducting its business. A sole proprietorship has never been held to be a partnership under the tax laws.

And, most important of all, the contractual companies are not trusts under the Code—for trusts, by their very definition, at common law, require a division or split of title (legal and equitable) between the trustees, serving on the corpus of the trust, and the beneficiaries.

Based on all of the above it is determined that the contractual companies created by contract, with Nassau Life Insurance Company, as trustee, are foreign fiduciaries taxable as foreign individuals under the Internal Revenue Code of the United States. The Internal Revenue Service has been aware of the existence of similar companies for many years, yet has failed to promulgate any regulations, revenue rulings, or other guidelines which mandate a different result. The foreign fiduciary (Nassau Life Insurance Company) is charged with the Management of assets, for a period of time, over which it holds full legal and equitable title in fee simple. As will be seen hereafter, provided that such full ownership is recognized, the oldest adage of the law comes into play—"Income from an asset is always taxed to the owner." Thus, the special tax laws applying to foreign nonresident individuals must be applied to the companies *unless* the I.R.S. can prove domicile in the United States, for business purposes, *or* company income "effectively connected with U.S. trade or business" as contemplated by specific tests spelled out by the I.R.S. Code or Revenue rulings interpreting same. While the reach of these two concepts, which sometimes impose U.S. taxation, will require a future opinion letter on the subject, it is safe to say the rules have no application unless a company has physical presence within the United States or *sources* of income in that country.

Much has been made of the "grantor trust provisions" already alluded to above, in other opinions by so-called tax experts, laymen or otherwise.

(See letter of April 23, 1983, Financial Freedom Consultants, W. L. Comer, Trustee, and letter of June 24, 1983 Copenbager and Copenbager, Attorneys at Law.) Both of these ill-reasoned opinions concede that which is not only unobvious in this area but extremely disingenuous—i.e. that one can apply grantor trust provisions without having a grantor or even a trust! Mr. Comer makes much of the "E.S.P. experience" in his analysis. He was apparently part of that "unfortunate" episode. Not surprisingly, an entity in which the taxpayer was both grantor, trustee, and beneficiary was rejected as "no entity at all" for tax purposes. This was due to the lack of separate existence, de facto, and, further, the impossibility of engaging in business at arm's length with one's self. In short, the Internal Revenue Service did not need to utilize the grantor trust provisions to defeat the "family trust" concept previously espoused by Pip Marshall Boyles and W. L. Comer, Et Al.

This so-called trust lacked an essential characteristic which your contractual company does not- —i.e. an adverse trustee found in the separate corporate existence of Nassau Life Insurance Company. The trustee of the contractual companies is not subject to the control of the holders of beneficial interest certificates but, instead, is bound only by the trust agreement. The adverse trustee holds full legal and equitable title to the assets "in corpus." When the contractual trust agreement is read in conjunction with the opinion of the United States Court of Appeals for the Ninth Circuit in Stern v. C.I.R.; No. 83-7177, the non-application of the grantor trust provisions, to this entity, is even more clear. The Court of Appeals noted, in Stern:

> "The trust instrument also allowed Sidney Stern to *remove the trustee without cause,* provided that he concurrently appointed a qualified successor trustee." See <u>Stern</u> at P. 3.
>
> "...Verra held a limited power of appointment and the power to remove the trustee...." See <u>Stern</u> at P. 4.

In holding for the taxpayers, the United States Court of Appeals for the Ninth Circuit makes it clear that even a power to remove the trustee is not alone sufficient to invoke the application of the grantor trust provisions even if they otherwise apply. And, of course, <u>Stern</u> involved a true trust with division of legal and equitable title between the trustee and beneficiaries.

Likewise, any fears that the contractual company would founder on the "doctrine of merger" or the "rule against perpetuities," are likewise groundless since the trust organization, formed under the contract, as already indicated, is not a conventional trust to which this doctrine or rule applies.

In light of the above principles, it is expected that the main thrust of any I.R.S. attack on the tax benefits will center on the "sham entity" theories expressed in <u>Moline Properties, Inc. v. C.I.R.</u>, 319 U.S. 436 (1943) and fully examined, in a manner favorable to the taxpayer, in <u>Perry R. Bass</u>, 50 T.C. 595. In our present case, a taxpayer who transfers property to the foreign contractual company through its foreign fiduciary trustee has placed the real, rather than fanciful, ownership of assets in the hands of an adverse party to be managed according to the specific terms and conditions of the trust indenture or agreement. He receives, in turn, beneficial interest certificates and must, thereafter, satisfy himself with the trustee's performance of his office in strict conformity with the terms of the agreement. This act by the taxpayer is voluntary and contractual in nature and, in effect, exercises the free choice of form within which to do business expressed, in the Moline decision, as follows:

> "A taxpayer may adopt any form he desires for the conduct of his business and the chosen form cannot be ignored merely because it results in tax savings. However, to be afforded recognition, the form the taxpayer chooses must be a viable business entity, that is it must have been formed for substantial business purpose *or* have actually engaged in substantive business activity."

Reference is made, once more, to the admission of Karl K. Krogue in the Dahlstrom case and the Court's instructions in Brownlee. The above test is one-pronged—meaning satisfaction of either of the alternatives is sufficient. Therefore, if a taxpayer can prove that he transferred his property into the corpus of the contractual trust organization, for a substantial business purpose or, thereafter, the contractual company actually "engaged in substantive business activity," then the attempted I.R.S. application of the "sham transaction or entity" theory is completely thwarted. This is exactly what happened in the Bass decision, where the taxpayer prevailed. Numerous other decisions, where the taxpayer adequately documented both his intended purpose for the formation or initial relationship with the foreign entity, and its conduct of substantial business activity thereafter, reach the same result.

The Tax Court notes:

> "Whether a corporation is carrying on sufficient business activity to require its recognition as a separate entity for tax purposes is a question of fact and Petitioner had the burden of proof. We think Petitioner met the burden."

See Bass at P. 600. The valuable lesson to be learned here is that each case will turn on its own facts and the more documentation or evidence the taxpayer engenders in his own behalf, prior to audit, deficiency, or trial, the better. Thus, anyone utilizing the trust company concept for foreign tax planning benefits should "over-document" each transaction journalizing their purpose for doing same, and encourage the trust organization, through its trustee, to establish as much business presence in the foreign domicile as possible. This means, ideally, mailing address, office, and actual on-site agents and employees, providing an array of services including accounting, investment, and legal. The challenged corporation in Bass had significant stature in Switzerland and could establish more than a mere "post office box presence."

An examination of related cases is even more informative. In Elvin v. Jones, 64 T.C. 1066 the Tax Court sustained the Commissioner's asserted deficiencies which attacked the separate tax status of a court reporter's corporation based, chiefly, on the "non-assignment" of income provisions contained in the Code. In a noteworthy aside, the Tax Court observed:

"There was no written transfer of the intangible asset which generated the income for
the corporation; i.e. the certification of the
transcript, because it could not be transferred."

See Jones at P. 1078. This passage seems to
approve and even applaud the transfer of income-producing property to the entity later challenged as a sham by the I.R.S. It is also in keeping
with the oft-quoted adage, already noted above,
that taxation follows ownership of income and
ownership of income would, per force, follow
ownership of the asset generating it.

Many of the cases after Bass display the mixed
results of I.R.S. efforts to disregard, for tax purposes, corporations utilized in tax planning by various taxpayers. In a scholarly opinion, Judge
Simpson of the United States Tax Court, dis-
missed the rationale of the I.R.S. challenging separate treatment of the corporate entity with the
following words:

"When a corporation carries on business
activities, the fact that the owner directs all
of its affairs, provides all of its assets, and
takes all of its profits makes no difference
for tax purposes."

W. C. Hudlow, Jr., T.C. Memo 1971-218 at page
941. As Judge Simpson also judiciously observed:

"The business which an officer conducts for
a corporation is not *his* own business; a corporation and a stock holder are separate
entities."

See Hudlow page 943. Citing Dalton v. Bauers, 287 U.S. 404 (1932) and Ralph E. Wilson, 40 T.C. 543, 550 (1963). Obviously, the implications between the above language and the operation of a contractual trust organization through its United States agents should not be overlooked. Both Hudlow, Dalton, and Wilson support Nassau Life's utilization of United States agents, to conduct U.S. business *without adverse tax consequences accruing to those agents.*

In analyzing some of the probative facts which might satisfy the tests of "conducting substantial business activities" the tax court, through Judge Forester, allowed that:

> "The salient fact is that Forum, Inc. was validly incorporated under Maryland law on March 29, 1967, and it engaged in substantial business activity. . . .

> "The record is clear that petitioner and Sullivan actively traded as 'the Forum, Inc.' at least until March 1969. Forum, Inc. had its own active checking account, contracted in its own name and otherwise held itself out to the public as a corporate business. We cannot ignore its corporate existence."

See Donald L. Schuerholz, T.C., Memo, 1976-163 at page 717.

The battle for recognition of separate corporate existence, for tax purposes, ebbed and flowed for many years until, at last, the I.R.S. despaired, appealed to Congress, lost the appeal, and then shut-up. Decisions like Foglesong v. C.I.R., 621 F.2d, 861 (C.A. 7, 1980) and Britt v. United States, 431 F.2d, 227 (C.A. 5, 1970) buried these

I.R.S. aspirations forever.

I.R.S. concentration on control of a corporation by a few individuals, was analyzed, and rejected by tax court Judge Tannenwald who observed:

">...If the element of retention of control were considered the determining factor, no transfer and lease barrier between the corporation and its share holders could be sustained. Any such tenet would raise havoc in situations that otherwise have all elements of a normal commercial transaction and fail to recognize the realities of the use of the corporate structure in the business world, namely, that 'policies and day-to-day activities are determined not as decisions of the corporation but by [the] owners acting individually.'

"While control cannot be totally ignored its presence in the circumstances of this case is not in and of itself determinative of unfavorable tax consequences."

Preston W. Carroll T.C. Memo 1978-173 at page 733 and 734.

By similar analogy, it makes no difference that one trustee (Nassau Life Insurance Company, Limited) is responsible for the business decisions of the trust or that only a handful of persons received beneficial interest certificates in exchange for valuable property. These factors, alone, will not support the imposition of the "sham" theory.

Last, in the corporate area, we examine the decision by which all other foreign tax planning cases, involving corporations, should be measured. The I.R.S. challenged a glove manufacturer's efforts to form a Bahamian corporation and, to establish a manufacturing concern in the Philippines, utilizing the corporate entity. The I.R.S. not only disallowed the valid expenses of the operation but, also, attempted to impose "a fraud penalty" on the entrepreneur. In a far reaching opinion, rejecting the specious and outright dishonest tax claims of the government Judge Simpson noted:

"We hold that the respondent has failed to prove by clear and convincing proof that Mr. Ross committed fraud. Contrary to the respondent's contention, the evidence does not show that Mr. Ross ignored or misinformed his attorneys or accountants. Two of his accountants testified at the trial and their testimony indicated a rather complete knowledge and general approval of the operation of Carla Trading and the arrangements in the Philippines.

"The respondent contends, however, that Mr. Ross had a plan to evade Federal Income Taxes and points to the different representations made in the Philippines and in the United States, Mr. Ross' allegedly personal use of the profits of Carla Trading and the incorporation of Carla Trading in a 'tax haven' country. It is clear that the representations made by Mr. Ross in the Philippines differed from those made in the United States, but it is also apparent that those made in the United States for the most part, accurately reflected the true state of affairs. In

any event, there has been no showing that
Mr. Ross ever intended to mislead the respondent. His 1962 discussion with the respondent's agent shows that he fully dis-
closed the nature of his operations. The
alleged personal use of funds by Mr. Ross
simply did not take place. The bank accounts
in the Philippines were those of Carla Trading
and were not used for Mr. Ross' personal
benefit. Mr. Ross' children were stock holders of Carla Trading and the findings of fact
clearly show the bona fide nature of the ad-
vances which he made to his mother on behalf of his children and the repayment of
such amounts to him out of Carla Trading
dividends on which his children paid Federal
Income Taxes. As manager of the children's
property, Mr. Ross pledged their stock as
collateral for loans which benefited Carla
Trading. Mr. Ross' attorneys did not suggest
that a formal guardianship was needed, and
we reject the respondent's contention that
the lack of a guardianship indicates that Mr.
Ross owned all of Carla Trading stock and
personally received and used the dividends
for such stock. *It is also clear that the establishment, in a 'tax haven' country, of a bona
fide corporation with a valid business purpose cannot be considered to be an indica-
tion of fraud on the part of Mr. Ross.*"

Ross Glove Company v. C.I.R. 60 T.C. 569 at
page 608 and 609.

The persecution of Mr. Ross bears an alarming
resemblance to the campaigns of government vili-
fication by misinformation described in Brownlee
above. In any event, the tax court soundly rejected

the I.R.S. attack on legitimate foreign tax planning. Ross demonstrates that something more is required to brand a taxpayer with fraud other than lost revenue or bureaucratic ambition.

Last, in this vein, even in Horvat v. C.I.R. T.C. Memo 1977-104, a case dear to the hearts of tax bureaucrats everywhere, due in large part, to its rejection of "family estate trusts" as tax planning devices, the tax court judge carefully points out that the taxpayers' form of trust planning was rejected due to the "anti-assignment of income" doctrine. As the court noted:

> "While most of the authority cited by petitioners is simply inapposite, petitioners essential contention is that they were in fact servants or agents of their respective family trusts, and therefore, the income is properly taxed to the trust....

> "In Bass this court held that a viable business entity actually engaged in substantive business activity cannot be ignored. That rationale does not extend to the facts presented herein. Similarly Scofield v. Mauritz, 206 F.2d, 135 (C.A. 5, 1953), wherein partnership interests were transferred to a trust, does not extend to the transfer of petitioners' personal services.

> *"It is clear that the services performed and the business activity conducted was that of petitioners and not the respective family trusts.* The very language of the trust agreement supports this conclusion as petitioners conveyed their respective family trusts 'the exclusive use of their life time services and

the resulting remuneration.' Petitioners and not the family trusts control the earning of the income. *Petitioners herein have conceptually failed to perceive the difference, albeit at times slight, between the anticipatory assignment of income to some other entity and the performance of substantial services by an entity through its agents or employees."*

See Horvat, page 484.

Under Section 1491 of the Code an "excise tax" is imposed on certain transfers of property by a "U.S. citizen, resident, domestic corporation, partnership, estate, or trust" to a foreign corporation, for paid-in capital, or to a foreign estate, foreign trust, or foreign partnership. This tax, in the amount of 35% of the "appreciated value" of the property transferred is the "tax contrivance of last resort" for I.R.S. agents attempting to impose tax liability on exchanges of property for beneficial units of the contractual company. Supposedly, this Section is applicable to all transfers of property in exchange for unit certificates.

On close examination, the attempted application of this "excise" section to the transactions previously described (in which the Trustee exchanges units for property) fails to pass muster. The first barrier to imposition of the tax is the already stated tax truism that values attendant to a transaction must be "readily ascertainable" before tax liability will become fixed. This is a principle governing all federal taxation—including income, estate, gift, and excise taxes. In other words, the value of the units given in exchange for the property must be "readily ascertainable" in order to fix and ascertain the present value of the property transferred. And, as previously explained, since the units represent only the right to a pro rata share of any distribution, if made, and the Trustees are not required to make any distribution, the fixing of valuation must wait until such time as the distribution is made at some uncertain time in the future. This contingency, in turn, defeats any effort to impose the thirty-five percent tax, as the valuation of a transaction, for tax purposes, must be fixed before a percentage of the value of the transaction can be calculated and collected.

Additionally, it should be further noted that Section 1492 of the Code excepts from the application of Section 1491 exchanges defined under Section 367. This Section, in turn, addresses contributions to corporate capital and defines transfers of property in exchange for corporate shares as "exchanges" and exempts such transfers from excise tax liability under certain conditions. See also Sections 1001 and 1002 of I.R.C. exempting exchanges involving property "of indeterminable value" from taxation.

Furthermore, as has been previously noted above, a contractual company is most analogous to a foreign individual. In the absence of statute or appropriate regulations or revenue rulings specifically dealing with the underlying facts and circumstances of the fiduciary contract, the claimed treatment of the contractual company, as a foreign individual is as legitimate as any. And, of course, the foreign non-resident individual is not named in Section 1491.

Further, in order to collect the above tax, the Internal Revenue Service would have to prove that the income of the contractual company was not "effectively connected with the conduct of a trade or business within the United States (and) is not includable in gross income under Subtitle A" of the Code. This argument would be self-defeating as, in pressing such a claim, the Internal Revenue would concede the tax benefits flowing from utilization of the trust forever afterward and would be limited to collection of the one-time "excise" fee, even if it prevailed.

Perhaps this is why the Internal Revenue has allowed Section 1491 to lapse into disuse and has displayed little appetite for its enforcement. (See Section 7701 (31) of I.R.C.)

The Congress of the United States has recently repealed all withholding on "foreign" income *other* than that generated by the sale of real property. It would seem that Section 1491 conflicts with the new tax act and its continued viability is suspect.

Last, in order of consideration, are the estate and gift tax ramifications of the exchanges of property for shares already discussed. A gift cannot occur unless the donor (party giving gift) gives more than he receives from the donee (party receiving gift). Once again, since the value of the units received in exchange for the property is not readily "ascertainable" at the time of the alleged gift, no difference, upon which a gift tax can be imposed, can be calculated. It should also be noted that the tax law generally presumes an equal exchange between the parties, absent evidence to the contrary. As a practical matter, although the estate and gift taxes are "unified," it does not appear that significantly adverse gift tax consequences would occur as the result of such an exchange.

In a most recent case, addressing attempts to disregard the corporate entity the "shoe was on the other foot." Unfortunately for taxpayer, it did not fit too well. In Roccaforte v. C.I.R., Docket No. 83-6561 (C.A. 5, July 5, 1983) the taxpayer "turned the tables" on the I.R.S. and attempted to disregard the corporate entity of one of his own corporations. The Fifth Circuit, in rebuffing this effort, observed:

> "Our holding today is also supported by strong policy considerations. Closely-held corporations often function as agents or surrogates for their owners. Under Moline Properties, Inc. v. Commissioners, 319 U.S. 436, 63 S.Ct. 1132, 87 L.Ed. 1499 (1943) however, they are treated as separate taxable entities. If a taxpayer could, by the simple expedient of relying on characteristics common to all such corporations, avoid tax liability, the separate entity regime would collapse. To prevent abuse, the taxpayer should be required to show more than those agency attributes that arise naturally from ownership and control of the corporation— he should be required to show that an agency relationship could exist independent of such ownership and control. This is precisely what the mandatory fifth condition of National Carbide Corp. v. Commissioner, 336 U.S. 422, 69 S.Ct. 726, 93 L.Ed. 779 (1949) requires."

See Roccaforte at P. 5507.

The I.R.S. often takes inconsistent positions in litigation only to regret such injudicious actions later. For many decades the Commissioner sought determinations denying taxpayers depreciation deductions on what he termed to be intangible assets which had no "readily ascertainable" value. Although his efforts generated mixed results, ultimately, it became a general principle of tax law that the values of a taxable transaction or event must be "readily ascertainable" before the tax may be imposed. This principle has far-reaching effects which were not originally envisioned by the Revenue Service. As noted by the United States Court of Appeals for the Second Circuit in Conde Nast Publications, Inc. v. U.S., 575 F.2d 400 (C.A. 2, 1978):

> "The Court held that because there was a transfer for an amount wholly indeterminable at the time of the transfer and only a part of the cluster of rights making up the copyright was transferred, there was no sale for capital gains purposes."

See Conde at P. 404. The Second Circuit in Conde cited another case with approval, Leisure Dynamics, Inc. v. C.I.R., 494 F.2d 1340 (C.A. 8, 1974) an Eighth Circuit case which reversed the decision of the Tax Court in Leisure Dynamics, Inc., T.C. Memo 1973-36 which denied the taxpayer any depreciation on the value of his "Gumby doll" franchise or royalties. While the Eighth Circuit ultimately found such royalties or franchise rights to have a value "readily ascertainable" enough to support a depreciation or current deduction, no indefinite contingency, such as that posed by the Trustee's discretionary rights to distribution was present. Both Conde and Leisure Dynamics strongly support the general principle that where the values in a transaction cannot be calculated, then neither can the tax.

This letter and opinion are written solely for

the use of Nassau Life Insurance Company, Limited, its agents, and subsidiaries. The legal opinions expressed herein constitute advice to no other parties other than those named in this paragraph. Other interested parties reading this letter are advised to consult their own independent counsel in determining their respective individual tax consequences which might arise as a result of their utilization of the foreign tax planning principles described herein. Furthermore, no attorney, or any other party, can guarantee the results of litigation. No guarantees are made of the results of any future litigation which addresses the principles already discussed or the opinions herein contained.

Kind regards.

Sincerely,

Joe Alfred Izen, Jr.
Attorney for Nassau Life
Insurance Company, Ltd.

Testimony in Brownlee Case

The following are partial excerpts from the transcript of direct testimony by Internal Revenue Service agent Lafferty, during questioning by Nassau Life Insurance Company, Ltd. attorney Joe Alfred Izen. Also included are comments by the Federal District Court judge and his instructions to the jury in U.S. v. Brownlee, which was decided in favor of the defendant and against the Internal Revenue Service.

Lafferty — Direct

A   I told them I believed the trust as presented by Traves

Brownlee was a sham.

Q   You did?

A   Yes, sir.

Q   And you distinctly remember giving that qualification in any statement that you made to, for instance, Mr. Schmidt?

A   I don't know if I qualified it.

        MR. IZEN: May I approach the witness?

        THE COURT: Yes, you may.

BY MR. IZEN:

Q   I direct your attention to a Memorandum of Interview in re Martin Schmidt, which states that present were Martin Schmidt, taxpayer, Robert Amato and John Lafferty, Wednesday, November 8, 1983.

A   Yes, sir.

Q   I call your attention to the second page where there is some writing of mine which you can ignore. I would like you to read that and see if you can refresh your memory, sir.

A   (After reading) Yes, sir.

Q   It is a fact that you told Martin Schmidt on that day that the trust was a sham, and there were no qualifications in that statement, correct?

A   I told him that the Chappell—Brownlee trust was a sham, yes, I did.

Q   Mr. Lafferty, a sham means that the trust never existed, correct?

A   No, sir, that is not correct.

Q   That wasn't your intent in telling this man that the trust was never a legal entity and that people couldn't enter into transactions with it?

A   No sir.

Q   Did Mr. Schmidt seem to be quite upset and scared at that time when you gave him this information?

A   No, no, he didn't.

Q   As a matter of fact, Mr. Schmidt always insisted throughout all your interviews with him that the trust was illegal? Right or wrong?

A   Wrong, sir.

Q   As a matter of fact, he insisted that the trust was legal, didn't he, throughout all your interviews with him?

A   Yes, sir, he did.

Q   Now, as a Special Agent it was your duty to determine how this tax planning, or whatever, functioned because you did investigate the trust benefits that people were claiming from the tax claim, is that correct?

A   Correct.

Q   As a matter of fact, leveling with us, the Internal Revenue Service thought at one time it might prosecute everyone that set one of these trusts up just for the fact they would claim the trust was a sham, is that correct?

A   I have no knowledge of that, Mr. Izen.

Q   You don't?

A   No, sir.

Q   So you are telling the jury and the Court that your investigation with all the conferences you had with Mr. Morris, Mr. Schmidt, and these others, was merely confined to the backdating of these receipts and the false returns of Mr. Dunning and Mr. Betlyon?

A   That was the crux of the investigation, yes, sir.

Q   So as far as the way in which the trust functioned, the Internal Revenue Service today is not challenging the fact that a trust can be set up, an individual can enter into transactions with the trust and generate deductible expenses on his own return, are they?

MR. CARPENTER: I object as irrelevant, as to what position different agents may be taking.

THE COURT: All right. I will sustain the objection.

BY MR. IZEN:

Q   What about your investigation, Mr. Lafferty? Did you attempt —

MR. MINNS: I am going to object to the ruling because it seemed like we sat here for a whole first day where they went over that trust, and it appeared to me that was an issue. If it is not an issue, I'd like appropriate instructions that all of the first day was unnecessary.

THE COURT: We better approach the bench.

(The following occurred at side-bar:)

THE COURT: Look, we sat in my chambers and everybody agreed that this wasn't an issue in this case. Now, I understand that things change from time to time during the trial of a case, but if something is material like that which has changed, I expect you to come and tell me about it. Is it an issue? I understood the Government was not claiming, did not intend to claim and indeed drafted instructions to expressly instruct the jury on this point, that the Government did not so claim.

Now, if that is the case and it is not in issue, this individual agent's opinion on this, I agree with the objection, it is irrelevant, and I will tell the jury that.

MR. MINNS: Let me give you my reason for objecting to the ruling. The credibility of this witness is at stake. This witness lied. This witness said that it was a sham when in fact he knew it was a legitimate trust. So that is the issue which we have a right to go into. The credibility of this gentleman is at stake and the credibility of the investigation. I intend to go into it in closing argument extensively, and I was hoping that Mr. Izen would be allowed to finish it so I wouldn't have to ask the questions, if this agent lied to people in order to coerce them into making deals.

I believe he lied to Mr. Betlyon in order to get him to confess to a crime he wasn't guilty of. That is at issue.

He has made two statements now under oath, one that he qualified it, and, two, that he didn't qualify it. I believe the truth is he didn't qualify it. I believe that the agent was dishonest, and I believe his credibility is at stake, and I believe originally Mr. Carpenter was misled because I believe he thought the trust—I believe Mr. Lafferty misled Mr. Carpenter in that area.

THE COURT: I don't understand how there could be a misunderstanding about this, but in case there is, there is nothing wrong and there is nothing in this ruling that implies that you cannot question this witness about anything that he told Mr. Dunning or Mr. Betlyon or Mr. Morris or anybody else, whether he threatened them with 37 years, whether he told them the trust was a sham, whatever—that has nothing to do with the question that was asked of this witness and was sustained, which was what the position of the Internal Revenue Service was with respect to the legality of these trusts.

MR. MINNS: I must respectfully disagree with the Court on that. If it is the Internal Revenue Service's position that it was legal, then that is impeachment evidence that Mr. Lafferty was lying when he said it was illegal.

MR. IZEN: Your Honor, my only point is this: I don't want a left-handed instruction where the Government says they don't contest the legality. I want it clearly established whether it is legal or not. It is true that this is a mixed question of fact and law from this witness, but I think it is really fairly implicated here that they undertook this investigation to do something specific against the trust, and then they convoluted it and turned it over to an easy case—I really believe it firmly happened that they were going to contest the trust.

THE COURT: If that happened in my view it is wholly irrelevant except to the extent it has to do with what was communicated or any pressure applied to these witnesses.

MR. IZEN: If the Court assures me it is going to give an instruction as to the legality of the trust entities, I can cut a lot of this short. I will simply rely on his credibility. But it is not enough from the defendants' standpoint, with the risk of 11 years in the penitentiary maximum sentence for the Government to say it doesn't contest it. My client wants me to get the truth out. If it is going to be posed as an issue unclear in law to the jury, I need to attack on that hand. If it is conceded that it is clear, I can eliminate a large part of my examination. So which is it going to be?

THE COURT: I understood that there was no objection to such an instruction.

MR. IZEN: You were going to instruct something to the extent that these trusts are legal entities just like corporations and other stuff, and I gave the Court an instruction from Domer v. Helry.

THE COURT: I intend to so instruct.

MR. IZEN: Thank you. I will be governed accordingly.

(End of side-bar conference.)

MR. IZEN: May I approach the witness again?

THE COURT: Yes.

BY MR. IZEN:

Q   With respect to the interview you had with Mr. Schmidt, was there any particular reason you instructed him that the trust was a sham?

A   He wanted to know what he was involved in. He said he has questioned the legality of it. So I told him exactly what I thought.

Q   That is what you thought at the time, that the trust was a sham, wasn't it?

A   Yes, sir.

Q   And you don't think that now?

A   I still think that, yes, sir.

Q   Have you received any training to the extent that it is proven that these trusts are illegal, that they are not entities?

A   I don't think you need any expertise to see how that trust as presented by Traves Brownlee is nothing but a sham.

Q   Well, you keep saying, "as presented by Traves Brownlee," back then with Mr. Schmidt, where you were at his doorstep and confronted him with alleged criminal acts, you don't make that qualification, do you, Mr. Lafferty?

A   As far as I knew, the Brownlee trust was a sham, and I was under the impression that that was the Chappell trust also.

So in my opinion both the Brownlee trust and the Chappell trust were a sham.

Q   You didn't make the qualification to him, did you, that it was the way Mr. Brownlee was presenting it that was a sham?

A   I told him, and I qualified it by saying, the trust is a sham. I didn't say it was my unqualified opinion.

Q   Mr. Lafferty, you would agree, would you not, that Special Agents of the Internal Revenue Service have certain duties as to truth and justice as far as the investigations that you conduct, and you shouldn't inform a taxpayer that something is illegal when it is not, should you?

A   Mr. Izen, as far as I knew, and which you have seen so far, the trust as presented by Traves Brownlee was a sham.

Q   What I have seen so far? What are you talking about, about what we have seen so far?

A   Well, on the tapes, for example.

Q   You are saying that it was a sham to create loans, if there was a bona fide intent to pay interest?

A   If there was a bona fide intent to pay interest, no.

Q   You are saying it is a sham for people to recycle a loan, make an interest payment to the bank and borrow the interest payment back?

A   That is a very gray area, Mr. Izen.

Q   Very gray?

A   Very gray.

Q   How gray does it have to be to be illegal?

A   To create receipts for the sole purpose of taking deductions on a 1040 is illegal.

Q   But again, as far as Mr. Schmidt was concerned, you explained all this stuff fairly to him, didn't you, Mr. Lafferty, that all you were concerned with was the backdating of the receipts? That is what you are telling us?

A   I also told them that I was concerned about the bank method.

Q   Bank method?

A   Yes.

Q   Does that appear anywhere in this memorandum of interview with Mr. Schmidt?

A   I don't know, Mr. Izen, I don't have it in front of me.

      MR. IZEN: May I approach again?

      THE COURT: Yes.

BY MR. IZEN:

Q   These are all the memorandums of interview that I was handed by Mr. Carpenter, and I am certain there are no others.

A   That's correct.

Q   So point out to us, if you would, after you refresh your memory, what the information was that you were concerned about the banks.

A   When I made the statement that the Brownlee-Chappell trust was a sham, I was under the impression that there were two methods you could use. One was the bank method, and if that was undesirable, one was the receipt method. Both in my opinion were a sham.

Q   But again you said the recycling was a gray area. Were there other gray areas?

A   No, sir.

Q   It is a fact that it is not gray if somebody pays the interest flat out, they would get the deduction?

A   I am not an expert, but if it was a bona fide loan and a bona fide and economic purpose for it, no, that is not illegal.

Q   Are you telling the Court and this jury that you weren't assigned by the Internal Revenue Service to keep these trusts from being marketed as a trust planning device and to save the citizens of the United States who used it for legitimate taxes?

A   No, sir.

Q   You deny that?

A   That's correct.

Q   So you weren't trying to make a criminal case out of any area that was a gray area, were you?

A   No, sir.

Q   You don't make criminal cases out of gray areas, you
concentrate on areas that are black?
A   Yes, sir.
Q   Again, Mr. Dunning and Mr. Betlyon filed these returns claiming these interest deductions. Were you concerned
at all with their W-4 Exempt forms?
A   Yes, sir.

CHARGE OF THE COURT

THE COURT: Ladies and gentlemen, now that
you have heard all of the evidence that there is in the case,
and the closing arguments of counsel, it becomes my job
to talk with you about the law that you are obligated to apply
in this case.

Although you are the sole judges of the facts in
this case, you are duty bound to follow the law as I explain
it to you and to apply that law to the facts as you find them
to be. You are not to be concerned about the wisdom of
any rule of law I tell you about, whether you think it is a
good rule or a bad rule. It would be a violation of your sworn
duty as jurors to base a verdict on any other view of the
law than the one I explain to you, just as it would be a violation of your sworn duty as jurors to base a determination
of the facts on anything other than the evidence you have
heard in this courtroom.

Justice through trial by jury necessarily depends
on the willingness of each individual juror to seek the truth
as to the facts from the same evidence that you have all heard
in this courtroom and to arrive at a verdict by applying the
same rules of law, that is the rules which I will explain.

As indicated at the outset, you have been chosen
and sworn to try the issues of fact in this case presented by
the allegations of the indictment and the denial made by
the not-guilty pleas of the defendants. You are to perform
this duty without bias or prejudice as to any party. The law

does not permit jurors to be governed by sympathy, prejudice, or public opinion. The defendant and the public expect that you will carefully and impartially consider all of the evidence in the case that you have heard in this courtroom, follow the law that I give you, and reach a just verdict regardless of the consequences.

Now the law presumes a defendant in a criminal case to be innocent. The defendant, although accused with a charge against them; a defendant begins the trial with a clean slate and with no evidence against them. And the law permits nothing but legal evidence against them. And the law permits nothing but legal evidence presented in a court of law to be considered in support of a criminal charge. So, the presumption of innocence is itself alone enough to warrant a not guilty verdict unless you have become convinced beyond a reasonable doubt of a defendant's guilt after you considered—carefully considered the evidence in this case.

Now, it is not required that the government prove guilt to a mathematical certainty or beyond all possible doubt. That would be an unrealistic standard in the human world, but the test is nevertheless, a stiff one. The government bears the burden of proving guilt beyond a reasonable doubt, and a reasonable doubt is simply a doubt based on reason and common sense—the kind of doubt that would make a reasonable person hesitate to act. In short, I think this is the best way to put it, proof beyond a reasonable doubt means proof of such a convincing character that you would be willing to rely and act upon it unhesitatingly in the most important of your own affairs. Proof beyond a reasonable doubt is proof that you would be willing to rely upon it unhesitatingly in deciding the most important of your own personal affairs.

The burden, as I explained at the outset, to prove guilt, is also on the government. It never shifts to the defendant and, indeed, a defendant in a criminal case has no burden of calling any witnesses, producing any evidence or giving any explanations.

The government's burden of proof beyond a reasonable doubt extends to each element of the crime the government charged, and I will explain those elements to you in a moment. If after you consider the evidence you have a reasonable doubt as to any of those elements, it is your obligation, your sworn duty, to give the defendant the benefit of that doubt and find him or her not guilty as to that offense.

Now, with these general principles in mind, let's turn to this case. I want to review what the contentions of the parties are and then talk to you about the essential elements of these offenses. The indictment has five counts. Two of those counts charge Mr. Betlyon and Mr. Dunning with willfully attempting to evade taxes by filing a false return, claiming false interest deductions. As you have heard here, those counts are not before you and you only need to concern yourselves with Counts I, III, and V.

Count I alleges that Traves Brownlee and Faye Brownlee conspired together and with others to defraud the United States government by obstructing the Internal Revenue Service in the performance of its duties of ascertaining and collecting taxes legally due.

Count III alleges that Traves Brownlee willfully and knowingly assisted or advised Mr. Betlyon in the preparation and presentation of a false return.

Count V makes the same allegation against Mr. Brownlee, but the return involved is that of Mr. Dunning.

Now, each of these counts charges a separate commission of a crime and it's going to be your obligation to make a separate decision with respect to each of these counts. Moreover, with respect to Count I which charges both Traves Brownlee and Fay Brownlee with conspiring, you are going to have to make a separate and independent analysis of the evidence bearing on the guilt or innocence of each of the two and make a separate decision.

The fact that you may find one defendant guilty or innocent as to Count I should not control your verdict with respect to the other defendant. You have to make an independent judgement there.

You will note that I am going to give you a verdict sheet. That indicates the separate decisions that have to be made, the two decisions that have to be made with respect to Count I. One is Traves Brownlee. The other is Faye Brownlee, and with respect to the separate decisions, with respect to those counts, you will have a place to check either not guilty or guilty there.

Before getting to the contentions of the parties and the elements of these offenses, let me emphasize several things that this case is not about.

First of all, it is not about whether you approve or disapprove of any view or opinions which a defendant may have held or expressed about the tax laws or any other subject. The First Amendment of the Constitution entitles you, and entitles me to believe what we want to and to communicate our beliefs to others, and those rights include the right to disagree with the tax laws, to communicate your disagreement with the tax laws to others, and also it includes the right to counsel others in legal ways to reduce their tax liability. Now, the First Amendment of the Constitution doesn't entitle someone to advise another to commit, or to assist another in committing a crime, or doesn't entitle you to commit a crime yourselves. So its focus has to be solely on whether the specific crimes that are charged in these three counts of the indictment, and each of the elements of those crimes, have been proved beyond a reasonable doubt.

Secondly, this is not a case about whether or not ACT members should have filed tax returns. Nothing that you decide here is going to have anything to do with anybody's tax liability. The United States government has procedures and means of collecting taxes that are legally due which have absolutely nothing to do with the criminal justice system. As I said before, this is a criminal case. There are very specific charges, and it would be unfair for you to do anything other than consider the specific charges that have been made here, follow my instructions, and decide whether guilt is proven beyond a reasonable doubt as to those specific crimes.

Third, this case is not about whether a taxpayer should undertake transactions or counsel others to undertake transactions for the express purpose of reducing his or her tax liability. Each taxpayer in our country has the perfect right to do everything within his or her power to legally reduce his or her tax liability to the least legal limit that can be reached.

Finally, and I suspect you will be glad to hear this, this case is not about the legality or propriety of contract trusts organized in the Turks and Caicos Islands or the deductibility of interest in fact paid on obligations owed to such a trust. There is no dispute in this case about any relevant issue of tax law. The government does not contend that the trusts were not valid legal entities, from the people who set them up or from those who held certificate units. Nor does the government contend that interest in fact paid to such a trust in satisfaction of an obligation to it is not legally deductible for federal income tax purposes. The government does contend, and the defendants agree, however, that it is unlawful to knowingly deduct interest which was not paid at the time one asserts that it was paid. It is not legal to knowingly counsel someone else to take such a deduction, and it is not lawful to work together with others to encourage such a practice or cover it up after it has occurred.

Now, the contention of the parties. The government in this case contends during the period from March to December of 1983, Traves Brownlee and Faye Brownlee willfully and knowingly conspired between themselves and with Dawn Henkel, Mr. Betlyon, Mr. Dunning, Mr. Schmidt and Mr. Morris. Now, the indictment alleges details about this conspiracy, and you will have it in the jury room with you. I just want to remind you, an indictment is simply a method of stating a charge. It is what the government claims it is. It is not evidence, and the only evidence is what you heard in this courtroom.

Now in summary, the government claims in the Spring of 1983, Mr. Brownlee and the people I have just named other than Mrs. Brownlee, got together and agreed to promote and utilize the foreign business trust concept as a means, not merely of legally reducing taxes, but of evading taxes which they knew were legally due. Specifically, it is claimed to be a part of the conspiracy or agreement that potential purchasers would be told that they could deduct interest payments which had not in fact been made, that purchasers would take such deductions, and that documents would be generated to make it appear that such interest had been paid. This would allegedly enable purchasers to secure a refund of taxes previously withheld and to avoid having any taxes thereafter withheld from their paychecks.

It is further specifically alleged by the government that this agreement and working together included the promotion and use of so-called old companies, which involved the backdating of the trust documentation so that it would appear that the company had been formed several years before the actual purchase of the trust services, and that this was done to permit the generation of documentation making it appear falsely that interest payments had been made in prior years.

Now, the government contends that during the course of this conspiracy, Mr. Brownlee had advised Mr. Dunning and Mr. Betlyon that, if they would buy a trust, they could generate 1982 deductions for interest which had not been paid, and thereby both secure a refund of taxes withheld in that year and avoid further withholding in 1983. It is the government's contention that after the trusts were purchased by Mr. Dunning and Mr. Betlyon, Mr. Brownlee helped them prepare their 1982 tax returns which claimed sufficient interest deductions to reduce the tax liability to zero. After these returns had been filed in June of 1983, the government claims that Mr. Brownlee assisted Mr. Betlyon and Mr. Dunning in getting documentation which would support these deductions and thus cover up the fact that false returns had been filed.

With respect to Mrs. Brownlee, the government does not claim that she was part of this conspiracy prior to the filing by Mr. Dunning and Mr. Betlyon of their 1982 returns in June of 1983. It is alleged that she later joined the conspiracy, or agreement, or worked together by assisting in the creation of documents to cover up the filing of the false returns, knowing full well that the interest claimed on those returns had not been paid in 1982.

Now, those are the government's contentions.

Mr. Brownlee contends that he was never a participant in any kind of agreement to generate conspiracy, or agreement to generate interest deductions of fictitious nature. He contends that he engaged in the legitimate promotion of the concept of a foreign contract trust as a tax planning device which would legally reduce the income and estate tax liability of United States citizens. He asserts that when he did this, he was under the understanding, based on his own research, and the opinions of various lawyers, that the trusts were valid legal entities and that interest payments to the trust on obligations to it resulted in a valid interest deduction which could be claimed on a taxpayer's return for the year in which the interest payment was made. Mr. Brownlee denies he instructed or advised Mr. Dunning or Mr. Betlyon to claim deductions for interest which they did not pay, and he further denies he participated in any effort to cover up the fact that interest payments had not been paid in 1982.

Finally, Mrs. Brownlee's position is that she was not originally involved with the trust concept, but that after a study of legal opinions and cases, and after a personal interview, going to the Turks & Caicos Islands, she concluded that tax trusts was a legitimate planning device. She contends she did not instruct or advise Mr. Dunning or Mr. Betlyon to claim interest they had not actually paid, and contends further that any assistance she rendered them in the Fall of 1983 was rendered without knowledge that those payments had not, in fact, been made, the claimed interest payments in 1982.

Alright now, to the elements of the offenses. Count I, as I said before, is a conspiracy count that charges both Mr. Brownlee and Mrs. Brownlee with violations of a federal statute which says if two or more persons conspire to defraud the United States or any agency thereof in any manner or for any purpose, and one or more of such persons do any act to effect the object of the conspiracy, each shall be guilty of such offense against the United States.

Now, a conspiracy is simply a legal word for a combination of two or more persons who seek, by concerted action, to accomplish some unlawful purpose. The gist of the offense is a combination or agreement or understanding between two or more people to disobey, or disregard what they know to be the law. Such an illegal agreement or understanding is considered by the law to be a crime separate and apart from any alleged crime that a co-conspirator may commit after the formalization of the conspiracy, and that is why Count I alleges a separate offense, an agreement, that has to be given separate consideration.

In order to secure a conviction for conspiracy, the government has to prove four things beyond a reasonable doubt with respect to the particular defendant you are considering.

First off, the government has to show that the conspiracy, like the one in the indictment, in fact existed at or about the time alleged.

Secondly, it has got to prove that the particular defendant you are considering at the time willfully joined in that conspiracy, or understanding, or agreement.

Third, it has got to prove that after there was an agreement or understanding toward an illegal objective, somebody did so act in furtherance of that agreement.

Fourthly, it has to be shown that the act was knowingly done in furtherance of the conspiracy.

Now in this case, the defendants are charged with

having conspired to defraud the United States by promoting a scheme which resulted in people taking fictitious interest deductions and by covering up the fact that such deductions had been taken. So, in addressing this first element, was a conspiracy like this in fact in existence, you have to determine whether at some time between March and December of 1983, two or more of those people alleged in the indictment to be co-conspirators reached an agreement, or understanding to promote such a scheme and to cover up its product.

Now, in making this determination about whether an illegal understanding existed, you have got to understand that the mere similarity of conduct between various persons, and the fact that they may have associated together and discussed common interests, does not necessarily establish the existence of a conspiracy or a particular person's participation in it. In other words, nobody should be found guilty of conspiracy on the basis of mere association with others.

Now, I said it is essential to show an agreement and that's really the heart of a conspiracy. It is not necessary for the government to prove that two or more of these people sat down and expressly wrote out what the objective of the conspiracy would be, or orally recited what everybody's part was going to be, but it is necessary that the government prove beyond a reasonable doubt that there was some common understanding reached, either expressly or passively, to pursue this illegal objective.

Turning to the second element that the particular defendant you are considering must have willfully become a member of the conspiracy, just as mere association is not enough to establish a membership in the conspiracy, so also mere knowledge that others are conspiring to an unlawful end does not alone establish membership in the conspiracy. You can know other people are conspiring without joining the agreement yourself. Evidence of association with others, and evidence of knowledge that other people are conspiring to an illegal end, is relevant evidence you can consider, but it is not alone sufficient, that the crucial question is whether a defendant willfully agreed to participate in pursuing this unlawful objective. When I say willful, I mean voluntarily and intentionally agreed with the specific intent to do something you know to be unlawful. So if a defendant with the understanding of the unlawful objective, or understanding, or agreement, knowingly encourages, advises, works with others to pursue the illegal objective, he or she becomes a willful participator, or what we call a co-conspirator, because that understanding of the unlawful nature of the agreement is necessary. A defendant in this case could not become a co-conspirator or willful member of this conspiracy without the knowledge that the trusts were to be used or had been used to enable the purchaser to take deductions for interest which had not in fact been paid.

One who willfully joins a conspiracy after its existence has the same responsibility as if they had started out at the beginning. Once you join a conspiracy you are responsible just as though you had been a member of it all along.

Moving to the third and fourth elements. The indictment in this case alleges that a number of overt acts were undertaken by alleged members of the conspiracy to further the objective of this alleged conspiracy, and you cannot find either defendant guilty unless you find that one of those acts was in fact knowingly engaged in by one of the co-conspirators for the purpose of furthering the conspiracy. In other words, you need an agreement plus one act. You don't need an illegal act. Any one of the overt acts stated in the indictment would suffice. It may be as innocent as walking across the street, or making a telephone call, or filling out a document, but there has to be an overt act. It has to tend to further the objective of the conspiracy and it has to have been done voluntarily and intentionally, and not because of some mistake, or act, or some other innocent reason.

Finally I go to Count III and IV. That I think is the simpler concept. The statute here reads:

Any person who willfully aids or assists in, or procures, counsels, or advises the preparation or presentation under the Internal Revenue laws, of a return which is false as to any material matter shall be guilty of an offense against the United States.

The government must prove three elements here beyond a reasonable doubt.

First: That Mr. Brownlee assisted or advised the preparation or presentation of a false return.

Secondly, that at the time he did that he knew, he had actual knowledge, that was false.

Thirdly, that he gave that advice or assistance willfully.

With respect to the first element, that is that Mr. Brownlee must have assisted or advised for the preparation of a false return, a false return is simply one that is untrue when it is made, and one that is known to be untrue by the person who is making it or causing it to be made.

The second element, there has to be actual knowledge of the falsity of the return that was filed. You can't find Mr. Brownlee guilty under Count III and V unless you believe beyond a reasonable doubt that he actually believed the returns to be false. It is not enough to show that he may have suspected that the returns may have been false.

Finally, it has to be proven to your satisfaction that Mr. Brownlee acted willfully, that is voluntarily, and intently, with a specific intent to do something he knew to be a violation of the law.

Now, you as jurors, are going to have to evaluate the witnesses that you heard from the stand. You are entitled to consider the manner in which they testified; the opportunity they had for observing what they had testified to; whether they appear to be giving truthful testimony; whether their testimony is consistent or inconsistent internally or within the context of all of the other evidence in the case;

what interests, if any, they have in this matter, in the outcome of this matter; and any other fact which you think bears—that you have heard in this courtroom that you think bears upon how much weight should be given to a particular witness' testimony, and you are entitled to give each witness' testimony just so much weight as you think it is worth.

Now I spoke of people having an interest being something you would want to consider. The testimony of an informer who provided evidence against a defendant for some personal advantage should be examined and weighed by the jury with greater care than the testimony of an ordinary witness who doesn't have that interest. So the bottom line is, you have got to determine whether the informer's testimony had been affected by his interest in that personal advantage.

As I told you at the outset, and this is very important, the law does not compel a defendant in a criminal case to take the witness stand and to testify or give any explanation or any evidence. Accordingly, you must not draw any inferences from the fact that Faye Brownlee has elected to invoke her rights under the Fifth Amendment of the United States Constitution, not to testify. There are many reasons that a defendant decides and elects not to testify which have nothing whatsoever to do with the issues of guilt or innocence. Indeed, the underlying purpose of the Fifth Amendment is to protect the innocent. You are not to conjecture or try to guess what the reasons or motivations may be here, and you are not to draw any inference from Mrs. Brownlee's assertion of her constitutional rights. You are not to speculate about things not in evidence.

What you are supposed to do is look solely at what is in evidence and say to yourselves, has the government proved each of these elements beyond a reasonable doubt. Your verdict must represent the considered judgement of each of you. That is, you have to reach a unanimous agreement before you can check the answers to these questions. When you return to the jury room to consider the evidence, I ask that you consult with one another with a view, and that you deliberate with a view, to reaching an agreement if you can do that without violence to your own individual judgement. Each of you has got to decide the case for yourself, but do that only after an impartial consideration of the evidence with your fellow jurors and after listening to their views.

In the course of your deliberations, don't hesitate to reexamine your own views and to change your opinion if you become convinced your own view was incorrect, but only—I don't want you to surrender an honest judgement as to the weight and effect of the evidence solely because of the opinions of your fellow jurors or solely so that you can return a verdict. Keep solely in mind that would be a violation of your sworn duty to base a verdict on anything other than what you have heard in this courtroom. Each of you are judges, judges of the fact, and your sole interest is to seek the truth from the evidence in this case.

The verdict sheet will be in the jury room with you. When you have reached a unanimous agreement with respect to the questions on here, your foreperson, who by tradition in this court is Juror No. 1, will fill in the verdict sheet and each of you will have an opportunity to sign it and you will return it to the courtroom.

That completes my instructions.

Chapter XV

Conclusion

The total disregard of the rights and freedoms of the talented individuals in the U.S. by those who called themselves liberals has proven to be one of the great fallacies in their notion that life could be made better by controlling all aspects of existence. Not only have talented individuals been unable to produce, and to create new means of producing, they have been forced into utilizing their talents just to regain their right to exist in an atmosphere of freedom.

As U.S. Congressman Dr. Richard Armey would say, "435 idiots in the U.S. House of Representatives does not equal one genius."

Dr. Armey has further said, "It is in fact the market that regulates the economy." Bureaucrats on the SEC, FTC, IRS, FDA and a host of other agencies thought not only that they could regulate the economy but that they were actually doing it.

The greatest example of this ill-informed regulation could be found in a statement by the chief of the enforcement division of the Securities and Exchange Commission who stated that the purpose of the SEC is to "maintain the integrity of capital markets."[1]

Not only did the SEC fail to maintain the integrity of capital markets but it destroyed them, as one can readily see

---

[1]Tape lecture series on Bad Times Breed Bad Ideas.

from the condition of the stock brokerage and banking industries. The good, the productive and the moral were penalized while the sure losers were being rewarded. This enforcer was in power during the period of time when the tax shelter (the sure way to lose money) came onto the scene. It was during this time when the SEC could walk into a federal court with any scrap of paper and get an injunction against a company. The issuance of an injunction was a certain doom for that company.

Since the injunction could be issued without the consideration of intent, materiality, or reliance, the SEC had dictatorial power to put anyone out of business. In my opinion that head of the enforcement division should be placed on trial with his freedom at stake. It should be determined if he in fact had the mental capacity to know what he was doing. And if he did knowingly and willingly destroy dozens or hundreds of companies for a badge, salary and government pension, he should be found guilty and incarcerated along with dozens of his co-workers.

The IRS now has this same power to obtain injunctions. If anything at all came out of the Nuremberg Trials it was that individuals have a moral responsibility to say, "No, I will not commit that act against my fellow man." Those in the IRS who are raiding the offices and violating every concept of the Constitution regarding constitutional or civil rights must be held accountable for their evil acts.

The market in fact has flexed its muscles, after a long period of tolerance for the great liberal experiment of controls, to declare its freedom and its power to regulate the economy.

This book would not be complete without mentioning John Maynard Keynes and his philosophies of controlling the economy to prevent the sharp ups and downs within it.

At best, his most popular theory of pump priming only half worked, as the staggering national debt of the U.S. reveals. The federal government could always pour massive amounts of money into the economy and stimulate it. This is the half of the theory that worked. The time did not arrive when the money, borrowed to pour into the economy in order to stimulate it, could be taken out to pay the debt.

Keynes, in the last paper he wrote before his death, reprimanded his followers for the extent to which they had carried his thoughts, ideas and theories. Each control had brought on the necessity for more and more controls. Keynes' theories were ones of control. Carried to extremes, one could not get out of bed in the morning and it would be illegal to stay in it.

John Kenneth Galbraith was one of the chief engineers of the era of destruction to the individual and the ruination of the first American Republic. I am told that students now boo him as they pass the door of his university office. It was Galbraith who stated:

> It doesn't matter how high the national debt becomes. We only owe it to ourselves. The American people are not intelligent enough to spend their own money; therefore, the government should take it away from people (through taxes) and spend it for them.

Galbraith must be given credit for renouncing this philosophy. When asked by an interviewer what he now thought about those statements, he replied, "We were wrong about that."

Hopefully, by now everyone who is a citizen of the USA will realize from the Supreme Court cases cited in this book that he and she have much more freedom along with more rights than previously realized.

The Supreme Court has been serving its purpose well with such decisions as:

> Anyone may so arrange his affairs to make his taxes as low as possible.

The legal right of a taxpayer to reduce his taxes
or altogether avoid them cannot be doubted.

The right to contract is unlimited.

But others, namely the IRS, your accountant and your lawyer, to serve their own ends, have been attempting to convince and persuade you that you do not possess these rights.

While these rights are yours they are not yours unless you recognize them and claim them. The disciple Mark in essence says in the Bible that you could be the wealthiest person on earth, but unless you have the faith to know that you have the wealth, you do not have it.

In order to have freedom it must be declared in one's head. Then one must exercise and put into practice that freedom which he recognizes himself to possess. No one can be mentally enslaved unless he allows himself to be enslaved.

Not only have attorneys and accountants attempted to capture and enslave your mind but so has the AMA, the educational system, religious organizations, your family and your closest friends.

However, since this book is about taxes, tax havens and protection of your assets, we will confine our discussion to attorneys and accountants.

There are many fine accountants and many wonderful attorneys who sincerely look out for their clients' best interests. However, in both fields they are rare. Fortunately, more and more attorneys and CPAs are recognizing that the time of the tax haven and the Contractual Company has arrived. We are experiencing at an increasing rate, attorneys and CPAs who not only arrange their affairs as recommended in this book, but they recommend the system to their clients.

Ronald Reagan, it appears, has read Fernand Braudel's books and perhaps consulted with Milton Friedman. Reagan recognizes the coming of the new era of the entrepreneur. As he said in his televised speech of May 28, 1985:

I believe in both spirit and substance our tax system has come to be un-American. For the sake of fairness, simplicity and growth we must radically change the structure of a tax system that still treats our earnings as the personal property of the IRS, radically change a system that still treats people earning similar income much differently regarding the taxes they pay, and, yes, radically change a system that still causes some to invest their money, not to make a better mousetrap, but simply to avoid a tax trap.

To deny that ultimately the government must repudiate its astronomical debt, brought about by Keynes' and Galbraith's experimentations, is a repudiation of common sense, which we not only brought onto ourselves but to the whole world and is always philosophically wrong.

If we compare the effects of a society living with great debt to a person with a severe toothache when there is a dentist nearby with the willingness and ability to alleviate the toothache, is it not morally wrong to live with the effects of the constant toothache? And is it not equally wrong to live with the pains and harmful effects of this national debt, knowing that ultimately the payment of the debt must and will be denied?

Assets must be protected not only from the IRS but also from the hordes of attorneys who will file suit against anyone without much cause who, in their terms, has "deep pockets" with anything at all in them. Someone has said that if one attorney comes into a small town he will starve; however, if two come into town they will both get rich.

The city of San Francisco has one attorney for each 108 men, women and children. Los Angeles has one attorney for each 134 men, women and children. This is a great overabundance when compared to the rest of the world, where there is no more than one attorney for each eight hundred people. The new slogan developed in California says "even attorneys need attorneys." Hopefully they will be suing each other and not the rest of the population.

As *Time* magazine observed:

> Legislative bodies have been spewing forth new laws at the rate of more than 100,000 in some years; as it happens, more than half of the members of Congress and one-fifth of the state legislators are lawyers. Federal agencies in the meantime are generating 35,000 or more new regulations every year. These developments have brought about a virtual revolution in American society: an all-pervasive invasion by courts, laws and administrative agencies into areas that had previously been ruled by custom, practice or plain old fashioned accommodation.[2]

Every year more than 30,000 new attorneys are pumped into the job market. U.S. Chief Justice Warren E. Burger says, "We may well be on our way to a society overrun by hordes of lawyers, hungry as locusts, and brigades of judges in numbers never before contemplated."[3]

Former Deputy Attorney General Laurence Siberman says, "The legal process, because of its unbridled growth, has become a cancer which threatens the vitality of our forms of capitalism and democracy."[4] Others wonder whether the rule of law will prevail in the U.S.—or the rule of lawyers.

In a television interview one young man told a story which may sound unbelievable, but similar situations occur daily across the nation.

A young couple had agreed to a divorce. They sat down at a table, each with a tablet, and wrote down how they

---

[2]*Time*, April 10, 1978.
[3]*Ibid.*
[4]*Ibid.*

would divide their furniture and other belongings. They had $25,000 in cash which they agreed to split equally. Each signed the paper agreeing to the property division.

At work the young lady was advised by a co-worker to see an attorney. The attorney said the paper the couple had signed was not a legal document. After the wife had hired an attorney, the husband felt that he must do the same. The bottom line to the story is that each attorney got $12,500 and all the couple had was their apartment furniture.

Chief Justice Warren Burger has said that he believes "as many as 50 percent of U.S. trial lawyers are incompetent."[5]

Chesterfield Smith, former president of the American Bar Association, has said that "he would not trust 25% of all lawyers."[6]

One can easily see that assets must be protected not only from the IRS, but also from attorneys. Many people believe that to go to an attorney and ask for advice about a problem which they fear might occur is a sure way to cause the problem to occur. The attorney will see to it, in some underhanded manner, that the problem will occur.

If a person hires an attorney to prepare a will, and if he discloses significant assets to the attorney, he is inviting trouble. In many instances the attorney will want to act as the administrator of the estate. The attorney may prevent the settlement of the estate from being completed for ten years or more. In the case of elderly people the attorney knows that if he can delay long enough, another death will occur and he can handle the estate of the mate of the first deceased person.

The offshore Contractual Company can adequately protect a person from the hordes of attorneys and perhaps prevent lawsuits from occurring.

If the attorney realizes that he is not going to get anything,

---

[5] *Ibid.*
[6] *Ibid.*

even if he wins a lawsuit, he is less apt to file the suit.

In any event the Contractual Company is the answer. *The power of contract is unlimited,* as we have seen earlier in the U.S. Supreme Court ruling on Hale v. Hinckle (Chapter VIII).

In the age of computers and high technology wherein new ways are evolving in all areas of endeavor, is it not logical that new and easier ways of conducting business should develop?

Surely, this book has revealed many ways of using the Contractual Company concept.

It has been said that any new concept in its process of evolution first meets passive resistance. In the case of the Contractual Companies, it would be attorneys and CPAs saying, "It may be alright, but I sure wouldn't do it." If the idea passes through the passive resistance, it then meets the hard resistance. This would compare to Nassau Life Insurance Company, Ltd.'s office being raided, a grand jury investigation, then later, a court test such as U.S. v. Brownlee.

If the concept survives and passes through both the passive and hard phases of resistance, it then becomes *the accepted thing to do.*

The Contractual Company, for asset protection, tax avoidance and estate planning, is becoming the accepted thing to do.

RESPONSE FORM

For further information regarding Nassau Life Insurance and its products, call (809) 322-8445, 322-8446, 322-8447, or 322-8448, or write or mail this response form to:

NASSAU LIFE INSURANCE, LTD.
FH 14547
Nassau, Bahamas

☐ I would be interested in additional information regarding offshore business entities.

Name _____

Phone (_____) _____

Address _____

City/State/Zip _____

Thank you for your interest.